Mark Chapman has been a professional(ish) broadcaster since 1996. He worked as a continuity announcer and cricket reporter (though not at the same time) before joining Radio 1. After a decade presenting the station's sport and cack-handedly DJing their weekend shows, he joined BBC Radio 5 live. Now a fully-fledged grown-up, he is the main presenter of *5Live Sport* as well as the *Monday Night Club*. Thanks to the wonders of make-up, he is allowed on television to present *Match of the Day 2*, as well as the BBC's Olympics, Rugby League and NFL coverage.

He lives in Cheshire with his wife and three children.

THE
LOVE
OF THE
GAME

THE AGONIES AND ECSTASIES
OF PARENTING AND SPORT

MARK CHAPMAN

WEIDENFELD & NICOLSON

A W&N PAPERBACK

First published in Great Britain in 2016
by Weidenfeld & Nicolson
This paperback edition published in 2017
by Weidenfeld & Nicolson,
an imprint of Orion Books Ltd,
Carmelite House
50 Victoria Embankment
London, EC4Y 0DZ

An Hachette UK Company

1 3 5 7 9 10 8 6 4 2

A CIP catalogue record for this book
is available from the British Library.

ISBN 978 1 4091 6329 9

Typeset by Input Data Services Ltd, Somerset

Printed and bound by CPI Group (UK) Ltd, Croydon, CR0 4YY

MIX
Paper from
responsible sources
FSC® C104740

www.orionbooks.co.uk

For my family

Acknowledgements

My first thanks should go to David Phillips and Tim Edwards, my agents at James Grant, who had been suggesting this would make a good subject for a book for at least two years before I got round to writing it. Maybe they were just bored of hearing about another Chapman family sporting weekend, and hoped that if I committed it to print it would give their ears a rest. Thank you to Rory Scarfe for then setting the wheels in motion and holding my hand throughout the whole process. Alex McGuire had the unenviable role of trying to organise that process, so thank you, too, for being, well, organised. Thank you to Alan Samson at Orion for liking the idea and being so enthusiastic at that first meeting. Thank you to Lucinda McNeile for patiently editing the book and making sense of some of the nonsense I have written. And thank you to everyone at Orion who helped publicise and market the book.

And finally, without sounding like an Oscar winner, my greatest thanks are reserved for my family and friends, many of whom appear on these pages. Mike, thank you for your contribution to this book. It matters so much that you took the time to write that section. Boney, thanks for being a great friend. I'm less grateful for having to play on the same team as you for so many years. Thank you to all those teammates over the years who have had to put up with me.

And then to Mum and Dad, Sara, Ben, Jessie and Millie, I hope this won't embarrass you now or in the future. Everything is done out of love, even though sometimes I may not show it.

Prologue

The bat I am holding is beautiful. Just beautiful.

I have kept and cherished it for twenty years. It still retains a lovely golden hue, so I obviously applied the linseed oil correctly when I was seventeen. The back of the bat has two hollowed-out strips that are painted red. If a bat was manufactured this way now, the marketing blurb would probably have us believe that this was to 'make it more aerodynamic and allow the ball to travel further' but back in 1990 such nonsense didn't exist, so it was probably done just to 'make it look nice'. Down the splice is a thick red stripe. Bat aficionados will immediately recognise, even from this very limited description, that the bat in question is a Gray-Nicolls. While my teammates were choosing Duncan Fearnleys, because 'that was the bat Ian Botham used', or Surridges, because 'Graham Gooch destroyed attack after attack with one of those', I went for Gray-Nicolls because it was endorsed by Michael Atherton. A swashbuckling batsman I was not.

And my blade gives testimony of my lack of swash and buckle. There is no big red spot slap bang in the middle where I once hit the fastest bowler in Lancashire for a six over mid-wicket. No tape applied to keep the bat together because I had wielded it with such power over the years – just several marks down the outside edge; evidence of numerous prods and pushes that invariably ended up in the gloves of a wicketkeeper or the hands of a slip. This day would be different though. Here I was in the summer of 2011, digging out the old bat and confident that at least today my power would come to the fore and I would crunch a few through the covers.

Having recently moved to North West England, I had been asked to go down to the nets of the local cricket club. With little else to do that day (the life of a sporting journalist isn't all go go go, you know) it seemed like a fun way to spend the morning and a chance for me and my playing partner to check out some sporting facilities in the vicinity. I said that I would drive us both down and so set about loading the car with our gear. In went my bat. I needed nothing more. Ten minutes later – after I had eventually managed to get his cricket bag, which is the size of a small wardrobe, a set of stumps, a change of clothes for after our session, two water bottles, a Powerade drink and a banana all into the boot (the banana didn't take up that much room but it has to be included, just to emphasise how much crap he needed with him compared to me) – we were ready to go.

It was damp, miserable and muggy as we set off to the club. It is always important when covering cricket to mention the weather conditions, especially when you are going to use them as an excuse for your performance later on. It was not a day to top up your tan. (Although in leafy Cheshire, it is normally a woman wearing surgical gloves and working in a booth who tops up your tan rather than the weather.)

Prologue

The rain was holding off as we pulled into the drive. I hadn't been here for twenty years and very little had changed. The drive was still a collection of sharp stones that could take out your tyre as easily as Michael Holding could an England batsman when I first started watching the sport. The pavilion might have had the odd lick of paint in the intervening years but nothing else had been updated. The first-team pitch, under covers, still had an untouchable air to it. I had never been good enough to get near it.

As we parked behind the pavilion, the nets were located to the right. Only three of them and they were all empty. In fact the place was deserted, which struck me as quite sad at the time but with hindsight turned out to be a blessing in disguise. As we got out of the car, I started to regale my companion with tales of my cricketing youth. He was suitably indifferent, plus he was struggling to carry all his drinks, the banana, the stumps and the small wardrobe over to the nets. I, on the other hand, was strolling over, twirling my cherished bat in my hand like a dandy. A twenty-first-century, sporting equivalent of Oscar Wilde.

The club was obviously concerned about people burgling the nets or maybe setting up a tent and squatting there, so before we could do anything, we had to negotiate the padlock. Once my companion had entered the code, we were nearly ready to go. We picked a net and I wandered down the AstroTurf to put up the stumps at the far end. It is always important when covering cricket to mention the surface of the wicket, especially when you are going to use it as an excuse later on.

The stumps were spring-loaded and all attached to one metal plate. As I set them down, I looked back up the strip to see my playing partner going through a stretching routine and moving his left arm round and round in a circular motion. *'He's taking* this seriously,' I thought. *'He might not be seeing this as just a friendly knockabout in the nets.'*

'What do you want to do first? Bat or bowl?'

Given he had been doing a passable impression of a windmill for the past few minutes I already knew the answer, but I thought it polite to give him the option.

'I'll bowl at you,' came the less than surprising reply.

I picked up my bat, turned on my heels and headed back towards the stumps.

'Do you want to stick a pad on?' he asked.

If you are unfamiliar with cricket let me just explain the role of the pads. Given that a cricket ball is a) very hard and b) can be hurled in a batsman's direction at some speed there are various bits of equipment available to the batsman for his protection: a helmet for the head, a box for the delicate areas and pads for the shins and the knees. When having a gentle 'net' a batsman might choose to forego some or all of the equipment and, at the level we were playing at that morning, there was certainly no need for a helmet or a box. The most that might be required would be one pad to protect my front leg, i.e. the one that would be nearest the ball. Being a typical man, I decided I would be fine without. I wasn't going to get hurt here, I really wasn't. I was going to channel my inner Atherton. That had to be good enough.

Even as I watched my opponent measure out his run up, I didn't think about protection.

He marked out ten steps.

'I'll be fine.'

Eleven steps.

'He isn't quick enough yet to hurt me.'

Twelve steps.

'I haven't got time to go and get a pad now.'

Thirteen steps.

'Remember, channel Atherton. Channel Atherton.'

Fourteen steps.

'If in doubt, just jump out of the way.'

He stopped.

'Thank Christ for that.'

He turned.

'Ready?' he shouted. He had to shout because he appeared now to be a very long way away. A cricket pitch is 22 yards long and he must have been that plus another 15 yards away from me.

'Ready,' I replied, while thinking: *'I am going to show him just what it takes to get to my level.'*

But just as pride comes before a fall, middle-aged bravado often comes before both mental and physical pain.

He began his run up. I gripped and I gripped hard the trusty old Gray-Nicolls. The greatest talents have soft hands. Mine were so tense the veins were bulging. I hadn't worn batting gloves either. I lifted the bat. I banged it into the AstroTurf next to my back foot. I lifted it once more as he got closer, my eyes focused on his run up. I was waiting to see the left hand gripping the ball. If you look at the grip as a bowler is about to bowl you can hopefully understand what he is going to try to do with the delivery. I saw the grip. I saw him begin the jump as he got ready to release the ball. I saw his right arm come out to try to give him some kind of accuracy. I saw the left arm get higher and higher. I saw him release the ball.

Then, I didn't see the ball.

I pushed forward to where I expected the ball to be. *'Inner Atherton: if in doubt a nice forward defensive will do.'* But I was too late. The ball had already careered off the pitch, grazed my knee and clattered into my stumps. If there was plenty wrong with my eyesight at that moment there was nothing wrong with my hearing, as I clearly picked up the noise of a wicket reverberating on a coiled spring, mixed in with the cheering of the bowler.

My head was down, I couldn't look up. I didn't want to acknowledge the delivery, give credit to the bowler or even look him in the eye. What I really wanted to do was rub my knee, because it bloody hurt, but I couldn't do that either because that would be a sign of weakness and also a sign of my own stupidity in not sticking a pad on in the first place. No, before I did anything I just needed to gather my thoughts together and that wasn't easy to do given the high-pitched mockery coming from the bowler. I've always found it quite hard to keep my temper in a sporting environment, but I had to remain calm here. I couldn't lose my rag because this was just meant to be a bit of fun. I also couldn't lose my rag because the bowler dancing a jig and gloating in front of me was my son. He was also eight years old.

Could I look up and blame my abject performance on the muggy conditions and the abject surface? No, I couldn't. Could I shatter his joy and elation by telling him he just got lucky and the ball might have hit a stray stone on the way through to me? No, I couldn't.

Instead I had to accept that I had reached a truly horrific stage in my life. The moment the sporting parent dreads. Holding the bat that I loved, that I was proud of, that had been such a part of my sporting youth and yet looked like a relic to my boy, I had to stand there, mainly on one leg because my knee was throbbing, and admit that it was over:

I was no longer better at sport than one of my children.

I had just been bowled all ends up by my EIGHT-YEAR-OLD son. Things would never be the same again. And that might include my knee.

Chapter 1

A comprehensive list of the great stadia in the world would be the subject of much debate and conjecture. It would probably depend on your choice of sport, your choice of team and your experiences in said stadium. Cricket lovers might throw in Lords or the Melbourne Cricket Ground; rugby union fans could suggest the Millennium Stadium perhaps; while the football goers could lob in Wembley. The football hipsters, after stroking their beards and straightening their skinny jeans, would probably opt for Borussia Dortmund's Westfalenstadion with its wall of noise and sea of yellow and black. I, and there is every chance I may be alone in this suggestion, would like to throw in Heywood Road, Sale.

'Ramshackle' wouldn't do the old place justice. There was just one area where you could sit, with wooden chairs laid out. To refer to this section as a stand would be taking it too far. In the rest of the ground you could just walk around and stand wherever you liked. Weeds protruded out of every nook and cranny and encasing the whole of the pitch was a railing, covered with chipped white paint and rust. At one end was a squash club, which actually made it way ahead of its time as a multipurpose sport venue because the main reason to go to Heywood Road was to watch rugby union: to watch Sale FC. They are now known as Sale Sharks after some marketing individual decided that they were prevalent in the canal that runs through the town.

I held my twenty-first birthday party in the stadium's bar. And, despite me somehow ending up with two ex-girlfriends giving daggers at each other all night and the hastily booked DJ ending the night with 'You'll Never Walk Alone' (which never tends to go down well in a suburban Manchester bar), I have nothing but fond memories of the place.

Before Sale was overrun with sharks and before I would even notice girls let alone have TWO exes, I used to go down to Heywood Road to watch the rugby union. For the casual adult fan it can be quite a difficult sport to understand, so as a child not yet into double figures, I found it particularly confusing. The saving grace was that this was before the rugby union authorities kept coming up with new rules every year, so there was a lot less stop-starting than there is now. To the untrained eye of my nine-year-old self, it simply looked like thirty men trying to whack the crap out of each other with the occasional bit of skill thrown in. This was also the era before groundsmen were invented so there was very little grass in evidence which meant that not long into each match it looked like thirty men all dressed the same trying to whack the crap out of each other with the occasional bit of skill thrown in.

I was always dressed the same as well. Rain or shine, hot or cold, my mum would send me wrapped in a cagoule. Every time I went I always had the same thing to eat too: a packet of salt and vinegar crisps. I used to place them in the pouch in the front of the cagoule, very much in the same way a kangaroo takes care of its young. It meant that I and the cagoule always stank of salt and vinegar crisps and means that, even to this day, whenever I open a packet of them and inhale the vinegar fumes it takes me back to the 1980s and Heywood Road.

The other constant in my trips to Heywood Road was my dad. There was always sport to be watched and if Dad and I weren't going to the football then we would go to the rugby. Into the brown Scirocco we would jump and five minutes later (on account that we lived quite close and not because my dad was speeding) we were parking up and walking into Heywood Road. There wasn't a ticketing system as such; my dad would pay on the gate and a man would hand over two raffle tickets as proof of payment. They were never checked and there was never a raffle prize to be won. As I walked past the ticket man there would be a welcoming nod while at the same time I could see in his eyes that he was thinking, *'Why has he got a cagoule on? It's a warm April day. And while we're at it, where is that strong smell of salt and vinegar coming from?'*

We never sat in the 'stand'. You didn't sit at rugby union games. It was about standing; all men together; drinking beer. Although not me and my dad. He was driving and I was nine. We always stood in the same place, on the far corner of the ground, opposite the entrance we came through. Sometimes I would lean against the railing, sometimes I would stand on the moss-covered concrete banks, ramped up behind the railing. That was as daring and as impulsive as it got because to describe the Sale crowd as creatures of habit would be a gross understatement. Men would stand in the same place every game, they would drink the same beer every game and to my young ear they would shout the same things every game.

We were always in the proximity of one man at Heywood Road. Dressed in a grey anorak with a flat cap protecting his bald pate from the elements, he always stood in the same spot and looked like the kind of old man us Sale youths would be encouraged to help across the road to prove we weren't young hoodlums terrorising the neighbourhood. Until he opened his mouth that is; because this was no frail old man. This was an old man who was going to stand in the same place at Sale every week and bollock every single player in blue and white, no matter who they were or who the opposition were.

Rugby union wasn't professional in those days. There was one cup competition, but aside from that every match was meant to be a 'friendly'. A succession of Northern teams would roll (literally, in the case of the physique of some of the players) into Sale. Orrell, Fylde, Broughton Park were often the opponents. Occasionally we'd get a bit of exotic glamour when a team from a far-flung foreign land would arrive, such as Neath or Boroughmuir. And then very, very occasionally we'd get one of the big boys such as Leicester. But the opponents were irrelevant to this old man. Sale needed criticising and he was the man to do it. And he was going to do it in a booming voice that you could hear on the opposite side of the ground.

'Mallinder, you're rubbish!' he would cry. Mallinder was Jim Mallinder, the Sale full back: a man who now coaches the rather successful Premiership side Northampton Saints.

'Smith, you can't pass it. You can't pass it, Smith.' He was keen to reiterate his point, but when he said it the second time he just cleverly switched the order of the words for a bit of variety. I am not sure Smith, who was Steve Smith, the England scrum half, ever really appreciated the subtlety.

'Stansfield, you are a big girl's blouse. A big girl's blouse that's what you are, Stansfield.' Stansfield was his favourite target. I don't think he thought he was particularly tough. He may not have been politically correct but this old man never swore. He was loud and he was critical but he wasn't foul-mouthed, so my dad was never concerned about standing near him. He amused us. He made us laugh and roll our eyes but after several games at Sale I wanted to know from my dad just what he was on about.

'Why is Mallinder rubbish? Why can't Smith pass?' and 'What is a big girl's blouse?' As I asked my dad these questions in the car on the way home and my dad gave his answers and put them into context, it dawned on me. This man next to me (I was allowed in the front seat for a short journey), this man approaching forty (that was very old in my world), this man who goes out to work in a suit, this man who drives me around, this man who shouts at me and my sister whenever we are naughty, this man who does a lot of DIY and gardening, this man, who does all of that, once used to be a sportsman. He actually used to play the game that we were watching.

My eyes started to sting with the tears that were forming. My breath had been taken away. This man was now a sporting super-star. He was no longer sat in a brown middle-market German car; he was bathed in the light of glory. My dad was a sportsman. He was a rugby player, not an architect. He would be the best dad in the playground, he would be able to shimmy and shuffle and score glorious tries against all of them. He was my hero.

That is the paragraph I would write if I had been granted poetic licence for this book. But I haven't. In reality, I did what every small boy does when they discover that their father has participated in some kind of sporting activity. I looked at him. I then looked him up and down, my young eyes drawn to the start of a middle-aged spread and said 'Really? *You* used to play rugby? *You* used to play that game that we have been watching at Sale?'

How could my old dad do some of the things that Smith, Mallinder and Stansfield were doing when he couldn't even stop me going past him and scoring a try in the garden? That surely wasn't possible. He couldn't catch me or tackle me, so he wouldn't be able to do that in a proper game, would he? The only person I had ever seen him tackle was my mum in a family game in the garden, and to be fair to my dad that had been a textbook tackle. That had probably been a clue that he had been a decent player, maybe still was, but at the moment it happened I didn't have time to think about it properly because he had tackled her with rather too much verve and vigour and the two of them had crashed through the fence into next door's garden. It was difficult to praise my dad as my mum tried to extricate herself from next door's shrubbery while at the same time threatening him with divorce.

Chapter 2

For the first Saturday in April it was a surprisingly warm morning. Cars and ambulances routinely trundled past on my left but I barely noticed them. The sun was shining through thin trails of wispy clouds and I perched on a bench and basked in its glow. I was also basking in the glow of becoming a father. Sitting there with my phone in hand, I was texting and telling as many people as possible that I was a dad. This was mainly through pride. I had a son and I wanted the world to know but also because I wanted to get back in to the hospital to check mother and baby were OK and then get home in time for Manchester United against Liverpool in the lunchtime kick-off.

The game would come later. Sitting on that bench, on 5 April 2003, I couldn't stop smiling. I had a son. I had a son. I had a son! We hadn't found out the sex of the baby before the birth and whenever we had been asked we had always said the right thing: 'We don't mind whether it is a boy or a girl as long as it is healthy.' And that was true but when he popped out – well, was pulled out with a plunger attached to his head because he was awkward is probably a more accurate description – I was overjoyed. I kept thinking sport, sport, sport! On that bench, in the sun, inhaling the passing traffic fumes, all the fun we were going to have raced through my mind. I'd be taking my son to games, just like my dad did with me. We'd be kicking balls about in the garden, I'd be teaching him how to hold a bat, putting on his armbands for the first time, showing him how to score in cricket, throw, catch, run and jump. We'd grow together in a specially built man-cave that would always have sport on the television and sporting games on the PlayStation. Nappies, feeds and sleepless nights hadn't even come into the equation by this stage. It was going to be all fun and no hard work. And before we go any further, I do realise I could have had exactly the same feelings if I had had a baby girl. And indeed my first daughter has proved to me that all those things I dreamt about doing and have done with her brother, she is determined to do too. She will not be left out and quite right too, but back in the spring of 2003 I was just excited to know I would now have a lifetime of father-and-son bonding ahead of me.

We didn't get off to a good start. Ben was three weeks old when we settled down to watch our first match together. A momentous occasion for a father. Less so for the child as they will never ever remember it. Even though there were just the two of us watching, I wanted to make sure he looked the part, so he had on his Manchester United babygrow as we settled down to watch United's game at Spurs. United were in a race for the title with Arsenal and there were only three games left in the season. It was tense, it was scrappy and there was little enjoyment to be had. The game wasn't much better. I couldn't get Ben to settle. He was restless, uncomfortable and cried a lot. We sat on the sofa, we walked around the room, we got close to the TV, we moved away from the TV, we went into a carrycot, we went out of the carrycot and we went out into the garden, although not too far because I still needed to see the screen.

Midway through the second half, we got comfy on a beanbag. United were 1–0 up and just needed to see the game out and they would be ever closer to another Premier League title. With my wife asleep upstairs and my son now asleep in my arms, United would hopefully be as serene as my current environment as they approached the full-time whistle. Time fades the memory so I can't actually remember whether the last fifteen minutes or so were nerve-wracking or not, but in the ninetieth minute Ruud Van Nistelrooy grabbed a second for United. Everything that happened next, though, is still fresh in the mind despite the passing of the years.

As the ball hit the back of the net, I cheered loudly, forgetting momentarily I had a sleeping baby in my arms. I also jumped up off the beanbag, again oblivious to the sleeping child. As I did, my foot slipped and the sleeping child went up into the air. Recalling my days fielding at gully (one of the closer-in fielding positions in cricket where you need lightening(ish) quick reactions), I didn't panic and calmly waited for Ben to land back in my arms, which he duly did and we watched the end of the game. Or maybe not.

In reality I flailed around, panicking that I was just about to drop my newly born son. I stumbled and slipped, my foot rammed hard into the Sky box, the television wobbled on its glass stand and, as the screen went black and I struggled to balance, I managed to grab on to Ben and prevent him crashing on to the floor. I now had a crying baby, a wife pelting down the stairs, a sore foot and a Sky box that wasn't working. Perhaps unsurprisingly an argument followed. I put it down to us all being tired and emotional with a new baby in the house as opposed to it being caused by my general lack of coordination combined with actually forgetting I was holding my son.

The argument spread to my mum and dad's house, two hundred miles away in Manchester. With Sky not working, a modern-day disaster for any sports fan, I needed to find out if United had held on for the win. The phone conversation went as follows . . .

DAD: 5 3 8 9 (never 'hello', always the last four digits of the phone number. I think it's a generational thing.)
ME: It's me.
DAD: Hi me.
ME: All OK?
DAD: All OK. All OK there?
ME: All OK here.
At this point Mum picks up another phone to join in the scintillating chat.
MUM: Hello. How's Ben? Is he OK? How's Sara? How are you?
ME: We're all fine. Dad, did United win?
DAD: Yep. 2–0. Were you not watching?
ME: We were watching and I saw the Van Nistelrooy goal but in celebrating it I jumped off the beanbag, slipped, nearly dropped Ben but caught him and in the process put my foot through the Sky box so the TV went black and I missed the end of the game so I didn't know whether it had stayed 2–0 or not.
DAD: So is the Sky box OK?
MUM: Jiiiiimmmmm!

The perception of friends and colleagues is that, as I work in sport, I must have rammed it down my kids' throats from an early age. The opposite has been the case, partly because I learnt from the previous incident that watching sport with a small child can be a dangerous business, and partly because if you force something on a child they tend to rebel against it. We decided early on that, although we would love all our children to embrace sport and its qualities, they had to discover it for themselves. Sport was more often than not on the television or on the radio but they wouldn't be made to watch it or listen to it with me, and anyway the bean-bag had been declared out of bounds by Sara for all future sporting activity.

There would always be balls around the house and in the garden, mainly because I wanted to play with them, but I would never demand that Ben kick or throw a ball with me. If he was going to I was adamant that it would be because he wanted to. I fought some quite strong urges to get him to kick a ball with me or play catch with me, not because I wanted a playmate or some father/son time but because I do believe that if you can throw, catch and kick a ball then as a boy your school days will be a damn sight easier. Rightly or wrongly, if you can join in those playground games or be part of a team to even a basic standard, there will be less chance of you feeling like an outsider. Less chance, to put it bluntly, of being bullied.

I did make him sit near me when Jonny Wilkinson dropped that goal. It seemed important, despite him being only six months old, but more often than not balls were pushed to one side and sport on the small screen in the corner was blissfully ignored. When Thomas the Tank Engine came on, however, he was slap bang in front of it, cajoling me to build him another track. Art, Physics and Craft Design and Technology were not my strong points at school, and yet my small son was expecting me to combine them all together on a daily basis while trying to avoid the shattering pain of kneeling on a Percy or a Gordon. Practice never made perfect but practice did mean I evolved in time from a rectangular track to a figure of eight. My track-building inadequacy was high-lighted whenever my architect father arrived and proceeded to engineer something that wouldn't have looked out of place in a window display at Hamley's.

A walk with Ben to one of the local parks would take us out on to the main road and over a local bridge, under which ran both Tube and overground lines. There was an eagerness on Ben's behalf on the way to the park as he knew that swings and slides and round-abouts awaited. If we timed it right at the weekends, there would always be a chance of catching a local amateur game of football or cricket. I can't just walk past a game going on in a park. I have to stop and watch, even if it is just for a short while. However, there was little interest from my son. There was impatience. He didn't want to stop and watch amateur sport, he wanted to get back to the bridge to watch the 'choo choos'. We must have spent hours on that bridge, right by a main roundabout, breathing in toxic fumes, watching train after train after train glide by. Ben would be sitting in his buggy, snuggled up in a big blanket and bobble hat waving profusely at every driver, while I would be bent down next to him, wondering if my knees had locked in the cold and if I was permanently stuck on my haunches. After much creaking and groaning – from my knees, not the tracks down below – we would walk back home; Ben happy and content, me wondering if I was doomed to a good few years' trainspotting with my son instead of a lifetime of sporting adventures.

But then something changed. It would be lovely for the pur-poses of this book if it was one romantic moment, that a bulb came on in his head and he saw the sporting light. If one day he picked up a ball and it glowed mesmerically as he held it in out-stretched arms with the palms of chunky little hands upturned. That classical music played in the background as he realised the power and the beauty that such a simple object could bring to his everyday life. That this one thing could be thrown or kicked, caught or headed, served or smashed, lobbed or dropped, and that because of it he would experience the full gamut of emotions . . . and that through being involved with this one object, this one beautiful ball, he would discover friends for life and create memories that would last forever.

In reality, he probably picked up an old tennis ball, held it high above his head, wobbled unsteadily as he tried to throw it, let it go and it bounced, rolled and trundled until it got stuck under the settee. This meant that I had to scrabble around in the dust and the crumbs under the settee (no point cleaning what you never see), with my backside in the air to get the ball back. And as any small child will tell you, putting your parents in an uncomfortable situation is a hilarious game and much more fun than getting them to build a train track, so Ben wanted to do it again and again and again. It is highly probable that the 'make Daddy fetch the ball' game turned him off trains and on to balls.

He was hooked. Thomas and Percy were forever parked in his little train-carrying case and balls were everywhere. At every opportunity he wanted to be in the garden or to be in the park; no longer did he want to stand on a bridge or a roundabout watching trains chug by. I found it exhilarating. To watch this little person, who I had helped to create, exhibit such a delight in sport and balls. I found it strangely emotional. If I was being completely honest, there was a sense of relief as well because, as I explained earlier, I thought that if I could get him to throw, catch and kick properly then hopefully his school days would be a lot easier. That was a big IF and also a big responsibility. Could I teach him the required ball skills?

Those early sporting years with any small child require an

inordinate amount of patience and also an unerring ability to put all your own instincts to one side and be unbelievably bad at all you are doing. I have had to carefully stage-manage any race, any game, any contest to make sure that in those early years my children always won.

I am one of the slowest individuals ever put on this earth and yet even I could beat all three of my children in a race up and down the garden; when they were toddling. So, as every parent will know, you need to develop your own technique that eventually enables this unsteady bundle of joy, energy and determination to beat you. I ended up developing a slow-motion running technique, and yes, I know, if you have actually been on a sports team with me you will say that it was my normal running technique but I was actually going even slower than that. Putting one limb in front of another would take at least five seconds to allow my opponent to get his chubby little legs ahead of mine. I imagined looking like a gallant runner in an epic film reaching for the line to claim glory, whereas in reality I probably resembled one of the lovers you see running down a beach into each other's arms in a cheesy romcom. Of course, small children are unsteady on their feet at the best of times so most races would involve one of them stumbling, at which point I would be left with a dilemma. Do I race past them and claim glory? The answer would always be 'no', but there is only so far you can take slow-motion running, and if I ended up going any slower I would be standing still. I couldn't do that as there would be a chance that as they picked themselves up they would recognise I was letting them win. The only thing to do when they fall is for you to fall yourself. The number of surprisingly tough daisies, dandelions and weeds I have tripped over is into the hundreds. And so while I am picking myself up and admonishing the offending small flower loudly for the benefit of my opponent, my child is running around, celebrating winning the race. And I am happy because we are having fun. I witness the joy and the elation on a small, ruddy face. I see the delight in them realising they achieved something in victory. I feel the warmth of family life and drink in the laughter and screams and whoops in the garden and tell myself to remember these moments because 'they won't be small for ever'. And yet all the while I am also thinking, 'Bugger, I've just been beaten by a three-year-old.'

Ben and I would spend hours both outside and inside playing a variety of sports. There wasn't just one thing he wanted to do, he was soaking up a variety of ball games and was keen to try them all. Football was prominent but cricket, tennis and rugby were all on his little agenda as well.

In those early years I found football the easiest to play with him. It was all very simple. I passed the ball to him. He passed the ball back. Eventually. It became slightly harder when he wanted to practise shooting. The power isn't quite there in a three- or four-year-old, which means as the goalkeeper you have to develop ingenious ways of letting the ball go in. I say ingenious; in reality, of course, I just mean falling over in a semi-comical, semi-realistic way. I became a combination of Norman Wisdom and Massimo Taibi. The ball would regularly go through my legs. I would have to dive over it using my speciality slow-motion technique, or I would rush out but miss both the ball and more importantly him and allow him a free run on goal. As the skills built up and the confidence and love for the game grew (in Ben not me) we reached the point where he would want a game. This would need careful stage-managing.

Our garden was not particularly big, but big enough for a father v. four-year-old son football match. At the far end of the garden, next to a small shed, we had a proper goal. Two nets would have felt extravagant and unnecessary so the other goal, the one nearest to the house, consisted of a bucket and a ride-on-sized Thomas the Tank Engine. Not so much jumpers for goalposts more children's tat for goalposts. Ben would always want to shoot towards the proper net as it was much more exciting for him to see the ball nestle in a proper net when he scored than it was to see it bounce off Thomas's plastic funnel and land by some wooden decking. The only negative in our arrangement was that it left me shooting towards the house and therefore shooting towards the windows. They shouldn't be in danger though unless I ever chose to thump a shot, but in a game with a four-year-old, there shouldn't ever be a reason to thump a shot, should there?

We would play first to five or first to ten. Ben would always win, of course, but it would be close. Always 5–4 or 10–9. He had to know that he had been in a battle with his old man. Watching him develop was another benefit of being a dad. He would try things he had seen on television even at this early age. Dragbacks, stepovers, nutmegs. They rarely worked, why would they? They hadn't worked for me for over thirty years so it was highly unlikely he'd nail them after only four. I allowed him the odd nutmeg (where a player puts the ball through the legs of an opponent and runs around him to take the ball) and resisted the urge to clatter him as he did it. The goals would be accompanied by celebrations; little dances, attempted cartwheels, shirts over the head with belly proudly on display. Ben would also sometimes celebrate his goals.

As fun as these games are, you have to remind yourself so many times in the course of them that you are taking on a four-year-old. Years of flying into tackles, hitting a ball as hard as possible and winning headers have to be forgotten. I had to allow myself to be tackled so that Ben could get the ball back, sometimes painfully as tackling hadn't really been on our radar and his technique was just to swing his leg and see what he could connect with. Ankle, shin, knee, ball: they were all the same to him. The old-school defenders of the 1970s and 80s would have looked on in admiration. If I went so near as to tackle him, he would roll around on the grass part screaming, part giggling. Children definitely copy what they see on television.

Occasionally the self-control would slip and I just wouldn't be able to resist the urge to let fly at goal. There were times in our garden, and I am not proud of this, when a small boy would stand still as a ball not only flew past his head but also hurtled towards the patio doors. Fortunately nothing was ever broken, neither part of my son nor part of the house.

I know I am not alone in my temporary enthusiasm to let fly. A friend of mine was in his garden playing cricket. His son was batting and after a good half hour of feeding balls for him to whack and then having to fetch them, my friend was resisting hard the urge to raise the game a notch or two. He continued, however, with his underarm throws and his son continued putting bat on ball, and, in the manner of a golden retriever in the park, my friend kept fetching the ball back. After a few more minutes of this monotony, he had had enough and wanted to do something different.

'I decided to give him a bit of chin music,' he told me.

Now chin music is a term that refers to bowling a ball shorter than normal so that it rears up off the ground and by the time it reaches the batsman is somewhere around head height – or I suppose chin height. Some of the best cricket footage around is of legendary fast bowlers tormenting some of the world's best batsmen with fast, short bowling: batsmen ducking, diving and jumping around to avoid being hit by deliveries that could be coming at them at speeds of around ninety miles an hour. Bowlers throughout the years from Truman to Ambrose, Holding to Donald, Lillee to Wasim Akram have used it as a weapon of fear and intimidation, and it has been witnessed at all the great cricketing venues of the world. It has not often, to my knowledge, been witnessed in a suburban garden in Middlesex.

Undeterred by the fact that the short ball is a weapon of fear and intimidation and knowing that he wouldn't be getting up to speeds of ninety miles an hour on account of middle age, my friend wound up his trusty right arm, and sent a tennis ball down his garden and past his son's ear. Startled and probably thinking that the ball had just slipped out or that his dad was just messing about, his son turned around and went to pick the ball up and throw it back to his dad. With the ball back in his hand, you might have expected my friend to have got his fit of pique out of his system. But no, he repeated the delivery. Again the ball whizzed past his son. Again it was retrieved. My friend now reverted to his underarm deliveries and allowed his son to hit the ball.

'He'll have to learn,' he said while recounting this episode to me. 'It won't be underarm throws throughout his cricketing life.'

'Absolutely not,' I agreed, 'although it probably will be for the next couple of years. He is only six, after all.'

'Never too early to introduce him to it though,' he added, unconvincingly trying to justify bouncing his small child. And while he stuck to that point, he decided to throw a couple of bouncers in there for a couple of other reasons, in my opinion. The first was to show his son that he could play cricket properly and that he wasn't just there to throw and fetch a ball for his son's benefit, and that in some way he would gain his son's admiration for being able to bowl a proper bouncer at him. The fact that, at that stage, this small boy had no idea what a bouncer was until that ball whistled past him, and that most people show no admiration for a person aiming the ball at their head, however old, let alone six, was lost on him.

Playing bat and ball with small children would test the patience of a saint. I have tried cricket, tennis and racket ball with my brood and all can be very, very hard work in the early days. Once again it comes down to coordination. Unless your offspring is Tiger Woods, who was driving golf balls with power and accuracy from the age of two, you have to accept that more often than not your child is going to be unable to put bat on ball.

Ben and I spent hours in the garden and on beaches on holiday with me gently throwing a tennis ball at him, him wielding a small bat, swinging in the vague direction of it, and then watching as it trickled past him with no connection made. He has given me thousands of looks to suggest it was my fault for not bowling it properly. He would of course expect me to fetch it and on the odd occasion he would do his own dirty work, the throw back to me would be so inaccurate that more often than not I would be spending a good five minutes trying to extricate the ball from a particularly thick bush. My main memory of those early days of playing cricket with him is of having a bad back through constantly bending down to pick the ball up or having to stretch into the undergrowth to retrieve it.

Tennis is even worse. Whilst playing that with either my son or my older daughter, the one word in the tennis lexicon that we never had recourse to use was 'rally'. Hitting the ball to each other was non-existent. The general pattern would be as follows: I would hit a ball over the net, Ben would run in, have a swipe and miss. I'd hit another ball over the net, Jessie would run in, swipe, connect with the ball with the frame of the racket and watch as it ballooned out of the court. And when I say out of the court I mean over the fence for Guess Who to go and fetch it back. I would always try to have at least three tennis balls in each pocket, as if I had some peculiar medical condition growing out of both thighs. I'd hit another ball, into the net. Another, way over my head. Another, missed. And so on and so on. I'd then go and gather them all up while the kids would run around, do cartwheels, pick their nose, basically anything to avoid the dirty work.

Those early sporting years are a slog, a test of patience and a test of your back. But all that pales into insignificance as you watch your children fall in love with sport. They develop before your very eyes. Fewer balls are missed by a bat, shots that you hit a bit harder are stopped by their little hands, you don't have to trip over that concrete dandelion quite so often. There is laughter and there are tears. There are cuddles and high fives and tantrums. There are walks back from the park caked in mud and soaked to the skin. Hot chocolates to warm them up in winter, cold beers to cool you down after a hot afternoon of rallyless tennis. Pure, innocent, unadulterated fun. Times that you know in your heart you will never get back because as they grow and they develop and as they drink in more knowledge and want to learn more and more, you know that kickabouts with Dad won't be enough. They want to be part of teams. They want to be learning with their contemporaries. The world of organised kids' sport is hurtling into view, and if you thought your patience was being tested in the garden, that's nothing compared to what awaits you.

Chapter 3

She came into the world hardly making a sound. There was a whimper as she was placed on her mother's tummy and her umbilical cord was cut. She had demonstrated some pace as well. One minute I was getting ready to read the sport bulletin on Radio One's *Scott Mills Show* while my wife was watching *Deal or No Deal*, the next I was at the hospital and cradling my new-born daughter before the ten o'clock news had even started. She had evidently decided that enough was enough and she couldn't bear to hear Noel Edmonds once again trying to convince us that what in essence is a game of luck and opening boxes actually takes strategy, nerve and tactics.

Wrapped in a white blanket, I cradled her while her mum slept. With our son Ben in my arms for the first time I had been thinking *'sport, sport, sport'*; with Jessica in my arms for the first time I was thinking *'Oh my God. A girl, a girl, a girl.'* As a boy, I knew more of what to expect with my first-born Ben, not everything but more. This beautiful, quiet little bundle in my arms would be a whole new experience. Every single step of the way there would be something new for me to get my head around. One boy, one girl. This was going to be a lot of fun.

Nature v. Nurture is a debate for a book a lot more highbrow than my own, plus it was not something that overly concerned the family. With one of each, two small children, and as every parent will recognise, it was more a case of getting through each day with all of us intact, some semblance of sleep and not driving each other mad, rather than worrying about if Jessie had too many pink things or whether we had made sure she had the same amount of books on diggers as she did on fairies. As with Ben, and as you hope with most parents with most children, as long as they were happy it didn't really matter what they were dressed in or what they were playing with. As long as it was safe. In fact the only time she played with something aimed one hundred per cent at the female market, she ended up in A&E. Quietly and without anybody noticing she had removed a month's worth of the contraceptive pill from her mother's bedside drawer and swallowed the majority of them. Rushed into hospital with a couple of weeks' worth of oestrogen pumping round her little two-year-old body, my wife was understandably panicking. Fortunately the doctor was calm and told my wife that she would be fine, there was no need for treatment and there would be no lasting side effects, because in reality all she had done was ingest a lot of female hormone. She was told there might be some mood swings in the coming days but nothing more. I am assuming he was referring to my daughter. For once I couldn't be blamed. At the time of writing this she is eight years old and I am hoping we have got our 'experimenting with drugs stage' out of the way nice and early in our father/daughter relationship.

Once we calmed down and recovered from the shock of what had happened, and before we continuously blamed ourselves for months afterwards, we asked Jessie why she had done it. I am not going to quote a two-year-old directly because you would probably find it too difficult to decipher, but to paraphrase her, she took them to copy her brother. She had seen him every morning at breakfast taking a vitamin pill and rather than sitting there like me thinking *'why are we buying vitamin pills, what a con and what a waste of money, why can't he just eat an orange?'* she was thinking *'I want to be like my big brother. I want my own vitamin pill.'* Coupled with the fact that on the odd occasion when the kids had seen Sara taking her pill, we had told them they were 'Mummy's vitamins', contraceptive being such a big word and a difficult concept for small children, so she therefore knew where she could get hold of some.

And that has continued throughout her life so far; not the pill popping, but the determination to match her brother. If he is doing something then she wants to do it, and not only does she want to do it but she wants to be better than him at it. I have found ever since having a daughter that there are no such things as 'male' sports and 'female' sports. Wherever we have gone and whatever we have been doing, both sexes have been participating.

She has undoubtedly been helped by having an older brother and having access to all the things he was playing with. Whereas he only discovered bats and ball at three or four, Jessie has been surrounded by them since being brought home from hospital. Even as her eyes were adjusting to the brightness of the world and colour was replacing black and white, balls were flying over her carrycot. Ben quickly realised that if Mum and Dad were busy and couldn't go in goal in the lounge, goal being an armchair at one end of the room, then the carrycot could be quite a useful keeper when placed against the base of the chair. He was oblivious to whether his sister was in it or not, it was just about working on his ability to chip the ball over the keeper (cot) and into the net (the seat of the armchair). Balls would hit her with regularity: sometimes it bothered her, sometimes it didn't. Sometimes we had to step in, sometimes we didn't. She got her own back when she was old enough to toddle but not old enough to be coordinated and wielded a variety of plastic golf clubs and foam cricket bats in the direction of her brother's head.

As the toddling became walking, and the walking became running, Jessie wanted to join in the games of football, cricket and tennis. Then you are left with an even greater challenge than those first games in the garden with just one child, when you are showing restraint and patience. Of course you still need restraint and patience because you are playing football with a six-year-old and a two-year-old but you also need the negotiating skills of a United Nations Secretary-General because a six-year-old cannot understand the need for patience with a two-year-old. You try to repeat all the old tricks that you used first time around but don't necessarily have the time to employ them, because there is an older child snapping at your heels taking it a lot more seriously.

I would be the keeper, encouraging Jessie to score a goal. She would have the ball halfway down the garden. She would start bustling towards me, the ball nominally near her, arms and legs, still encased in baby fat, pumping away. A mass of uncoordinated child coming towards me. The leg would kick out and often the ball would stay where it was, the foot having missed the connection. Slowly but surely, both she and the ball would inch towards me in the goal. I would start to open my legs so that she could eventually kick it between them, score the goal, and head off celebrating. She would be one kick from glory. The first kick would miss the ball.

'Unlucky, Jessie, try again.'

A second kick. A second miss. I would reach out my own foot to bring the ball closer so that now even the slightest touch from her would ease the ball through my legs and over the imaginary line and into the net.

'This is the one, Jessie. You are going to score this time.'

Back she went to take a big run up at this one and as she did she was clattered by her six-year-old brother who, having lost all patience, took both her and the ball in one tackle and ran up the other end of the garden to score a goal. This then left me with a crying child in a heap, shocked, maybe bruised and mightily annoyed that after all that effort she still hadn't managed to put the ball in the goal. It also left me with the dilemma of having to tell Ben off for knocking his sister over and not allowing her to score, while wanting to tell him how much I had admired his tackle, albeit one on a two-year-old.

As you move through the different stages of your life, things come into fashion and then quickly disappear again. Things that were important to you when you were a child mean absolutely nothing to your own kids. Cassettes, video recorders, phones with a circular dial on them, an A–Z, a phone book are all items that I have had to explain to my kids at some point or another, to be greeted by a look of incredulity. In the interests of not appearing too sad, I ought to point out that A– Zs were not important to me growing up, they are just an artefact that I have had to describe to my children. Bizarrely, phone books did actually play a part in my adolescence, as the first job that ever involved me receiving a wage was delivering the new edition of the Yellow Pages to my local area. We had to stack two thousand of them in my mum and dad's garage, before driving across the Altrincham and Timperley area, dropping them off. And you couldn't just leave it on a step, because that could signal that the householder was out. You had to ring the bell first of all and if nobody was in then hide it somewhere in their front garden. To this day, I get annoyed when a phone book is left on my front step. It doesn't happen too often. Also to this day, my mum and dad have copies of the 1991 Yellow Pages in their garage because I didn't get round to delivering them all.

There was now a new addition to my list. The local community hall. If you had asked me pre-children whether these buildings were still around, I would have struggled to have answered you on account of not caring one jot, and yet now, in the quest for some proper structured coaching for Ben, I was about to walk into the kind of building I hadn't set foot in for nearly twenty years. This time I would be walking into it in jeans, hoodie and trainers and holding the small hand of my first-born. In the early eighties I was walking into a similar building with a green cap, green jumper, shorts, socks, tawny woggle over my neckerchief and trying not to hold the hand of my mum.

Cubs took place every Wednesday night in a community hall attached to a primary school. All the boys were split into groups with the idea of working in teams, improving themselves as individuals and helping out in the community. A heart-warming and admirable philosophy that was encapsulated in the motto of Lord Baden-Powell's scouting movement: 'Be Prepared'. The majority of us just wanted to play football, which doesn't prepare you for a great deal, but is a damn sight more enjoyable than learning how to tie a reef knot or put up a tent. For every new skill acquired, you were awarded a badge, and that badge would be sewn on to your green jumper to indicate just how much knowledge and experience you were acquiring. I think in my three or four years of being in the 5th Brooklands and Sale Cub Scouting movement

I received three or four badges. A badge per year. And they were all to do with sport. Map reading, cake baking, clay modelling, sewing, whatever it was, didn't interest me. I was at this thing with my mates so just give me a ball. While the conscientious members of the pack went off to try to recreate the Leaning Tower of Pisa out of clay while simultaneously baking some chocolate crispies to take to the local old folks' home, the rest of us were usually involved in the wholly worthwhile pursuit of Crab Football. And yes, that is as literal as it sounds – football with the players participating in a position reminiscent of a crab.

The hall was too small and we were too big, even at nine and ten, to be playing football at full pace in the correct position. So the easiest way to still get a game going and to slow it down a bit was to play with us somewhat lower down. This wasn't unique to our Cub pack or our community hall. As astonishing as this may sound, Crab Football was commonplace in schools and halls across the country. Thousands of boys would regularly get down on the floor, put their hands out to their sides, push themselves up so they would be balanced on both their hands and their feet and then scrabble around the floor in search of the ball. You weren't allowed to shuffle on your backside, that could never touch the ground, and obviously you could only ever use your feet to touch the ball, never your hands. There were no goalkeepers in our games. The only saving grace was that you didn't actually have to move like a crab. You could go forwards and backwards as well as sideways.

And we wonder why my generation never won anything at football. Maybe we should have encouraged more international Crab Football tournaments? It was great fun, apart from the one time I lost control and went head first into the wall at one end and knocked myself out. Who knew that crabs could move so fast?

But aside from the fun and the laughs and the odd minor touch of concussion, it would be hard to argue that there was any other point to it. We might at a push have been learning teamwork, at an even greater push spatial awareness, though it is easier to find space when the boy next to you can't even balance on his hands and feet and takes two minutes to turn himself around. We certainly weren't improving as footballers and we weren't improving our skills.

So some twenty years from turning myself into a small crustacean for sporting purposes, I was now walking into a village hall with my son to see whether he would be putting himself through something similar. But of course he wouldn't be because times move on and things were not always better back in the day.

I walked with Ben through the double doors, coloured blue but with the paint chipped and fading. The internal door had a pane of glass in its centre, through which a stage was visible at the far end of the room. It was empty, with big thick heavy curtains draped on either side. There would be no performance there this afternoon. The floor was the stage for this afternoon's activity and if as a parent you wanted to stay and witness the performance then there were grey and orange plastic chairs lined up on the perimeter of the room for you to sit on.

The room was full of small nets, cones and balls. As soon as you were in the room the children were encouraged to leave your side and get stuck in. Very few needed encouragement to do just that. Off Ben went, kicking a ball, throwing a ball, catching a ball. There would be bumps and bruises and tantrums as two four-year-olds fought over one ball, ignoring the fact there were fifteen spare ones behind them that nobody was playing with. As we waited for the class to begin Ben would be dribbling, trying to pass to me and then shooting into an unguarded tiny net before running off celebrating with his shirt over his head. I'd then have to run after him to get his shirt back down because he couldn't do it himself and I didn't want a like-father like-son repeat and for him to knock himself out at the base of the stage. Those moments before the session actually began appeared chaotic but it was important chaos because it was allowing the children to become familiar with the balls, in any way they wanted.

These sessions were put on by a company called Little Kickers and they usually provided two or three coaches for a group of around twenty children or so. Coach Hal would lead the way and apart from the warm up every child would always have their own ball to work with. The children were aged between three and five so there was probably little need to warm up, except of course they had all seen the professional footballers warm up. Children do copy, whatever anybody says, so if Wayne Rooney was doing a hamstring stretch in a game they had seen that week then they wanted to do it in their own little way too.

With limbs 'suitably' warmed up, it was then all about encouraging their love of the ball. Not their love of football, but their love of working with a ball at their feet. The coaches weren't drilling them, they were coaxing them and cajoling them. Yes, there were cones for them to dribble around but if they weren't able to do that then they could just run with the ball and try to smash it into one of the small goals. Kids would bump into each other, balls would collide and go flying off in different directions, forcing children to go off in different directions, and through it all the coaches would laugh and praise and help. Never once did I hear a voice raised.

Now you might think that that is how it should be. Why on earth would a coach of a group of small children need to raise their voice? But that would be to assume that all children wanted to be there. And of course not all of them did. Little Kickers was my first experience, and certainly not my last, of parents using sporting clubs and organisations as a childminding service. For the past decade, every sport my children have done, every summer camp or half-term course they have attended, has been blighted by some kids not wanting to be there and only being there because it was a cheaper alternative to a nanny.

In those early Little Kickers sessions, Ben was oblivious to those who wanted to be there and those who didn't. He just wanted a ball at his feet and a net to blast it into. The majority of the kids there were the same. Coach Hal encouraged them every step of the way but as the sessions continued he started to introduce little bits of skill to try to punctuate them simply running from one end of the hall to another and scoring goals, over and over and over again. There was nothing complicated, most were only just out of nappies after all. It was simple stuff like trying to stop the ball while you were running by putting your foot on top of it. Then once you had mastered that, maybe stopping it and then turning and going back from where you had come from. This took time, of course it did, and once again balls would be flying off and getting stuck under pushchairs belonging to watching parents, but as I sat there over the weeks, I marvelled at how they were improving.

As well as marvelling I was also struggling to recall whether I had ever been coached in a similar way. Now, there are two reasons for this. The first being that I struggle to remember what happened last week, let alone something that happened over thirty years ago. The second reason is that I was struggling to recall it because I am fairly sure it never happened. I don't think that I was ever coached on how to do a skill. Ever. Now this is evident if you have ever had the misfortune to watch me play or have been a teammate, but whereas I was coached to head the ball, pass it and tackle, I was never coached to take care of it, to cherish it, to perform skills with it. My coaches could well have taken one look at me and decided that even if they had tried to teach me any of that, I was so gangly and uncoordinated that I wouldn't have been able to do it, but equally it just didn't work like that back in those days. This was the first time in my life, but it certainly wouldn't be the last, of watching one of my children learning skills that I hadn't mastered when I was their age and still wasn't close to mastering now.

As well as Ben being taught some skills at a very early age, there was another big difference between his first experiences of playing football and mine. He was playing with girls! I add the exclamation mark simply for emphasis and not for shock value. Every step of the way through his early footballing career, girls have been involved. From joining in in those early Little Kickers days to him joining an actual club, he has played with girls, against girls and been coached by girls. He has never questioned this. I have never heard his friends question this. Indeed, why should they?

They are reaching their teenage years now, where boys and girls go their separate ways in most sports, but up until now it has been largely integrated. Past generations make sexist comments about women in sport, my generation make sexist comments, my son's generation give me hope. Why is it important that they give me hope? Well obviously because it is the right thing to do but also because I have two daughters. Ben has two younger sisters and if they can't do what he does, have the same opportunities he does, they are going to be mightily pissed off. And so will I.

Chapter 4

'Ben, just let her score.'

'No.'

'Please?'

'Why?'

'Because you are winning 9–1. She is only two years old, she is tired, she doesn't know the score and just wants to score a goal.'

'OK, if I have to.'

I would then hold Jessie's hands above her head and swing her with the ball at her feet to give her extra momentum. We would progress towards Ben's goal.

'Now just let her score, Ben.'

'Yes, Dad.'

Once again the ball would be no more than a metre from the goal where Ben was positioned. I grabbed Jessie's hands, gave her a big swing and she connected with the ball.

'Just dive over it, Ben, or let it go through your legs,' I would think.

He would bend down, pick up the ball, gently lob it back over my head and run towards the other goal and smash it in.

'10–1, 10–1, 10–1.'

Tears, tantrums, shouting, exasperation ensued from both Jessie and me. Sometimes it was difficult to tell who was the toddler.

Then there was cricket.

'Just let her hit one, Ben.'

'OK.'

'No, don't take a big run up, just stand still and bowl under arm and allow her to hit it.'

'OK.'

He then proceeds to stand still as instructed, but as I stupidly haven't requested a pace to throw the ball at, he launches it with all his might at his sister who doesn't even see it, let alone hit it.

'Let's change it round. Jessie, you throw it and see if Ben can hit it.'

Then in a whisper to Ben: 'Just miss the first one and see if she can hit your stumps.'

'No.'

'Please?'

'OK.'

Ball leaves Jessie's hand, heading somewhere towards her brother holding a bat. Ball ends up in next door's garden.

I was fighting a losing battle. No matter how hard I tried to explain the need to soften, slow or moderate his own skills, pace and energy for his sister's benefit he didn't want to or understand the need to. He was only six, of course. He was also very keen to point out that sometimes both myself and his grandpa had forgotten to temper our own sporting behaviour, in particular during a family get-together to celebrate my mum turning sixty. Rather than have it somewhere convenient and local, it had been decided that we would all head to a hotel in deepest, darkest Hert-fordshire. Invited were my mum, not surprisingly, my dad, my sister and her partner Dave and myself, Sara and Ben. It wasn't that Jessie was barred from this gathering but more that she hadn't been born yet.

From the Friday afternoon to the Monday morning we stayed in a hotel that was beautifully quaint on the outside and would have made a lovely backdrop to a Miss Marple mystery, but was tired and old-fashioned on the inside. Saturday morning was spa morning for the girls which left my dad, myself, Dave and Ben on our own in the hotel grounds. Mindlessly walking about was not something any of us particularly wanted to do but we wanted to be outside rather than staying inside drinking coffee in an area reminiscent of a 1970s show home. So out came the rugby ball.

Now hotel gardens are not the easiest things to play sport in. They are well-manicured, well-tended areas of peace and beauty. They are designed to be enjoyed and looked at, not torn around by a group of men who should know better. They are full of trees, flowers, bushes, ornaments and water features. They are not full of cones, bibs, whitewash, posts and nets. They will often have a 'Keep Off the Grass' or a 'No Ball Games' sign attached to a wooden stake and neatly inserted into the grass verge by a path. The concrete is your territory, hotel guest, the lush green grass is out of bounds.

On this crisp autumnal morning, there were no signs. There were plenty of flora and fauna and there was a smattering of or-naments. Water features were noticeable by their absence. There was a pond, though not a particularly big one. It was maybe six foot by six foot and it certainly didn't dominate what was a large space to throw a ball around in. Which makes it even more sur-prising that we were drawn towards it to such an extent that we ended up playing rugby around it. Yes, we had run up and down the hotel lawns throwing the ball to each other, bumping into the odd apple tree, but that wasn't nearly as much fun as standing around a small area of water throwing a ball to each other. As there were four of us we could each stand on one side so we weren't going to get in each other's way and there was the 'jeopardy' of not knowing who was going to receive the ball next. There was no determined order. And just in case it has slipped your mind, because I'll be honest with you I think it had slipped our minds during this game, one of the people involved in this was just three years old.

The game was progressing quite calmly. Ben struggled to throw the ball the majority of the time but he managed to catch the odd one. Throwing one across the pond but leaving it just short so it splashed in the water and soaked the intended recipient would have been quite amusing except that it was a cold morning and the pond looked filthy, so there was an unspoken agreement that we wouldn't be doing that. The only time the ball touched the water was when Ben, with his little arms, couldn't quite carry the pond with one of his passes.

Dads doing what dads do then started to happen, which is to show off. Not me towards my son, but my father towards me. The tricks and skills of his youth started to make an appearance. He was flicking the ball out of the back of his hand, looking one way and passing the other, throwing it with extra zest, zeal and spin in my direction to try to make me look incompetent in front of my own son. He succeeded and my little lad lapped it up. He had Dad, Grandpa and Uncle all to himself. We were all laughing and joking and cheeks were rosy and he was wrapped up and happy and using all of that remarkable energy that small children have.

Then he fell into the pond.

My dad had hold of the ball. He and my son were opposite each other, the pond between them. Still in trick mode, he went to throw the ball to Ben, with a small amount of spin on it. He didn't get it quite right. The ball came out of his hands but with no pace on it whatsoever, so despite the fact that the distance between them was only around six feet, the ball did not look destined to reach the other side of the pond. Ordinarily this wouldn't have been a problem. In the course of the game several of the passes had landed in the dank, dark, slightly pungent water and we had just fished the ball out without worrying what bacteria were being transferred from leather on to human skin and then continued. The difference this time was that although the ball wasn't going to reach Ben, it wasn't just going to flop into the water. With incredibly bad luck it had just enough pace on it to land on the concrete edge of the pond. Given the shape of a rugby ball, it is not a friend of the regular bounce but on coming into contact with the edge it gently lolloped up into the air. Ben watched it gently rise up and thought '*I can catch this*', while simultaneously forgetting he was standing on a precipice. Taking one step forward, he kept his eyes constantly on the ball. I was very proud of that fact: coaches in any ball sport will always tell you to concentrate on the ball, keep your eyes on the ball, never get distracted. That advice would more than likely change if the pupil was standing by some water.

With that one step he went straight in, feet first. Splash.

It wasn't easy to fish him out. My eyes were stinging with tears of laughter. I know he's my son and he was only three and a half but it remains to this day one of the funniest things I have ever seen. His comic timing was not at fault. I wasn't helped by both my dad and brother-in-law being doubled up in hysterics as well. Ben, remarkably, found it funny too. He didn't cry, he wasn't laughing as much as the rest of us, but he wasn't upset. He was just cold, wet, dirty, smelly and slightly shocked.

His head hadn't gone underwater because the pond wasn't that deep, so once I had grabbed his hands and got him out it was back to the room to get him out of his clothes and into the bath. Within half an hour of him falling in, he was clean, warm and dry and the two of us were still thinking that this was the funniest thing that had ever happened. He liked the attention, the fact that it was him who had fallen in, while I couldn't lose that image of that one step, eyes on the ball and then in he went. He was back to not having a care in the world. I still had to tell my wife and my mum. It was not a conversation I was looking forward to but fortunately Ben was quite keen to tell his mum himself. With a deep breath from me and a grin from him we put the call in.

She was in the spa, a fact that I had forgotten in the chaos of the preceding hour, so it went straight to answerphone.

'Hello Mummy, I've fallen in a pond playing rugby with Grandpa and Daddy. Bye.'

Detailed messages are not a male Chapman speciality, and it seemed that Ben had inherited that fondness for brevity. For the rest of the weekend there were many knowing looks exchanged. Anytime we encountered water or went out of the hotel into the garden, I was asked whether I was going to allow 'our son' to fall in again. The rugby ball stayed firmly in the boot of the car and that was really his last taste of the sport. My dad and myself have pointed out on many occasions that rugby pitches don't tend to have a pond in the middle of them so he would be perfectly safe but it has had no effect. Rugby immediately became associated with danger in our house so it remained off the agenda, plus a couple of years later, once Ben had found his first proper football team to play for, he wasn't going to look back.

Chapter 5

How do you choose that first football team for your child? Not to support, but to play for? The majority of parents deliberate for a long time when it comes to finding the right school for their offspring. Are they in the right catchment area? Are they going to have to move to get into the right postcode? Are they going to have to consider the independent sector? I just assumed that Ben would be going to the local school around the corner from our house and didn't think much more about it. My wife was more diligent and put proper care and thought into researching the various options available and while she was doing that I took it as my duty to replicate her thoroughness when it came to the local football clubs.

We had plenty of options in the area of Middlesex where we lived. I was helped by my friend from university, Steven Bone: Boney was Harrow born and bred and had played football through all the junior leagues as he grew up. The club he played for was still going strong and having played football with Boney for over a decade by this stage, I immediately ruled his former team out of the running for Ben. If they had produced a 'footballer' like Boney, then I feared for their coaching! Also Boney's son, Joe, was playing for a different club, Harrow St Mary's. I had popped down a couple of times to watch Joe. The set-up was decent, nothing fancy. There was plenty of enthusiasm, kids didn't appear to be shouted at and it was close to our house. Like so many clubs up and down the country, in both junior and senior football, it was basic but it was warm and full of good intentions and if you could accept doing a sweep of the pitch for dog shit before training and matches then it was a solid, decent club for a young boy to start his footballing career in.

If there was one negative, and I appreciate the dog turd bit is a big negative for a lot of people but it becomes a way of life in underfunded grass roots football and you just get on with it, then it came in their choice of kit. White! Harrow St Mary's, from Under-7s all the way through to Under-18s, played in white shirts. Somebody with no concept of washing kids' kit came up with that. White is a great colour for football kits, it looks the business and indeed I know of teammates from my university days who would deliberately wear white shorts and socks in pre-season training. They reasoned that, having been on holiday, the white would perfectly offset their tanned legs and hopefully make them more noticeable to the selectors, and any girls who might have been passing. This was pre-David Beckham. Maybe Beckham developed his metrosexuality after a couple of summers watching Hull University's pre-season training? Whether that theory worked or not for the boys at Hull, white is not a colour for a children's football team. Particularly when they play on parkland with copious amounts of mud, in August let alone November. Shirts could probably last a team a couple of years and six months into them we would be telling opposition sides that we played in grey rather than white.

So, Harrow St Mary's it was, white shirts and all. That first Saturday morning approached. The week leading up to it loomed on the kitchen calendar. Even to this day, in this hi-tech world of ours, our family life is ruled by the kitchen calendar. There were nerves and concerns, worries and excitement, butterflies and the fear of the unexpected. The Friday night before was the most difficult. It was impossible to concentrate on anything else. Would too much energy be wasted by worrying so that come the actual day nothing would be achieved or accomplished? I've no idea how Ben was feeling but I was going through the wringer. As a parent, you spend the majority of your time in perpetual worry that you are doing the right thing for your children but this was causing me more angst than most decisions. And if you are thinking *'get a grip, man, this is just about choosing a football team for your son'* then maybe this isn't the book for you. But let me try to explain.

Stuart Dalgetty, Christian Purdue, Andrew Satchwell and Christian Hyland. Names that will mean absolutely nothing to you and yet these are some of my earliest teammates in football. I have no idea what they are up to now but when I look at a team photo from my school, Cub or club days I can name the boys in the line-up. What makes that even more remarkable is that I can do it even though we all looked the same, with the same bowl haircuts. I don't think wax or gel had been invented in the late seventies or early eighties. I can look at school photos from the same era and struggle to name anybody on them, unless I had played football with them. The happiest times were spent with these lads. Nothing to worry about, no idea what was ahead of us, we were just a group of boys kicking a ball around. We were being taught about friendship, teamwork and how to deal with things going wrong without even knowing about it. We were under the care of parents and men who gave up their time to make us happy and we probably never showed our gratitude. When not playing organised football, we would meet on the field at the back of my house and just have kickabouts. I don't want to get too nostalgic but during the holidays we would be out from early in the morning until late in the afternoon playing football, only stopping for food and drink. I realise I'm close to describing an idyll and that we climbed trees and had lashings of ginger beer, but I must be quite firm on the fact that while it was great fun I didn't live in an Enid Blyton novel. There were uncomfortable moments as well, such as when my dad decided to referee one of our games and wanted to send Stuart Dalgetty off for spitting. Not for spitting at my dad, or spitting at an opposition player, just for spitting on the grass. He didn't approve of this nasty habit, but even so it did seem harsh to want to send off a nine-year-old to ram home his message. After a lot of arguing, Stuart was allowed to continue for the rest of the match as a teammate of the referee's mortified son.

I wanted Ben to have similar experiences, minus embarrassing refereeing performances from his dad. To be able to look back many years later and remember his teammates and recall how they learnt the game together. To have his teammates over to have a kickabout in the garden, because we wouldn't be letting them stay out all day at the local field on their own. He would be making his first friends through football and learning how to win and how to lose. And that was why I wanted to make sure we got it right.

The Saturday morning arrived. Off we went as a family, the three of us, for Ben's first training session with an actual football club. We arrived at the park and saw a throng of parents and small children. Some parents eyeing each other up, some parents

chatting and familiar with each other, all the small children running around excited. We didn't really know anybody, so we just
stood to the side (a theme that could well become familiar as we
progress) and watched and waited. We sat Ben down and took off
his trainers and put on his brand new football boots. Brand new
boots were a novelty back then, though it feels over the years like
we have gone through at least three pairs per season.

Eventually the kids were all called together and off they went
with a couple of coaches. The parents were also called together so
that the ground rules could be laid down. 'Respect' is the key word
in junior football nowadays and that was rammed home in that
first chat and quite right too. Respect for the coaches looking after
your children, respect for your own child and their teammates
and respect for the referee when we eventually reached games
against other sides. This wouldn't be about winning, this would
be about developing the kids as footballers and as people. It was
an admirable philosophy and it helped that it was delivered by a
man who had been at the club for a couple of decades, so in the
course of that time he had seen and heard everything. There was
a lot of nodding and murmuring in agreement from the parents,
although even then you could see one or two doubting the philosophy. Surely football was about winning and also making sure
that your child became so good that they were taken on by a club,
became a professional footballer, earned millions and allowed the
parents to retire? It was going to be an interesting and probably at
times infuriating journey. And that journey was beginning right
now with our offspring crowding around a couple of coaches in
the middle of a park in West Harrow.

The chat had also encouraged us to make full use of the club's
small catering operation because that would help with the fi-
nances over the season, so with a bacon sandwich in one hand,

a polystyrene cup of steaming hot instant coffee in the other and the club's coffers swelled by £2, I went off to watch Ben's first-ever training session as part of a club.

The two coaches couldn't have been more than sixteen or seventeen; closer in fact to the ages of the children in their charge than the adults watching. The first session was as much to do with everybody getting to know each other as it was football. By the time we had walked over to where the group was situated in a far corner of the park, there was little evidence of football and plenty of evidence of mayhem, with small children running in all directions. One football had been left forlornly by the side of the pitch, a bag of balls untouched alongside it. Immediately you could sense the tensions among some of the parents.

'My child has joined a football club. He is meant to be doing football training. Why are the footballs in a bag? He should be scoring lots of goals. He should be showing everybody within a two-mile radius that he could be the new Messi. We didn't sign him up just to run around. What is going on?'

Twenty minutes or so into these kids' footballing career and already they were experiencing the less than helpful questioning of the sporting parent.

When I described the children as being on a pitch, I was doing a disservice to pitches up and down the country. It was a patch of land with faded whitewashed line markings just about visible through the slightly overgrown grass. There were no goals as such because all frames were flat packed and then built when required by coaches or helpful parents. For the first session, the children didn't need to be smashing balls into large goals, so a few smaller pop-up ones, no more than a couple of feet in width and the same in height, were scattered around the perimeter. Large orange and yellow fluorescent poles marked out the area the kids were running in, each one of them having a built-in spring mechanism so that if a child clattered into one it would merely bend with the force, rather than being an immovable object that could knock them out.

The children weren't running around aimlessly; well, they were, but the two coaches had tried to implement some kind of structure. They were encouraging the kids to play a game called Crocodile, designed to encourage teamwork, fitness and spatial awareness. To the untrained eye, they were playing tig. A couple of boys were wearing bibs, they were crocodiles, and if they caught you then that meant you had been eaten and had to stand round the outside of the area until there was a winner. A fairly simple game with fairly simple instructions unless you happened to be my son.

Within a couple of minutes of arriving to watch them in action, Ben was looking somewhere between confused and petrified. While the majority of the boys were running around, going hell for leather, Ben ponderously moved around the rectangle. He was shrugging in our direction and gazing pleadingly at the coaches. With a large group of children to keep their eyes on, he didn't catch their attention. His small steps came to a standstill, one of the boys in the bib touched him and so according to the rules of the game he had to make his way to the side. He just stood there and immediately I knew what was coming. The bottom lip came out, the eyes became moist and the tears began to well. Then he couldn't stop them. Half an hour into his first ever training session at his new club, my little boy was in floods of tears at the side of the pitch.

There now follows a difference of opinion in our household as to how the next few minutes progressed. I believe my heart melted as my son – bemused, confused, tear-stained and tiny

– stood on that field looking for guidance and help and that as soon as I saw that I just wanted to hug and comfort him and make everything all right. My wife will tell you that standing on the sidelines I became more and more exasperated.

'What's wrong with him? Why isn't he running around? Why has he now stopped moving altogether? Why is he looking at us rather than playing a game? Oh now he's been caught. He's got to move now. Oh no. Oh no. I think he's going to cry. The bottom lip is wobbling. Oh brilliant, he's now crying. Great. What is the matter with him?'

Those are just some of the words she has probably made up over the intervening years but has suggested came out of my mouth. Equally, she has a different version of events for when he was brought over to us for a bit of TLC. She was ready and waiting with a bear hug and a biscuit and a drink to try to get him back on an even keel. I was 'apparently' ready to tell him to get back out there and toughen up. It was just a game of tig after all and what would all the other children be thinking of him, now that he had cried during the first session. In my head I was there with the cuddle and the encouragement. I was there to put a smile back on his face and tell him not to worry because it was only a game and to explain the rules to him. Because that was why he had been so upset. He hadn't understood the rules. He didn't know where he could run, where he couldn't run, when he had to be inside the posts and when he was meant to stand out-side them. He was just a baffled little boy. Once everything had been explained and he had calmed down, he rejoined the group with a big smile on his face, a smile that didn't leave him for the rest of the session. Dribbling, passing, shooting and a big game at the end were all participated in without one more tear being shed. His mum and dad on the other hand spent that whole time on the sidelines, away from the other parents, arguing about their differing reactions to his earlier predicament.

Looking back, Sara's version probably holds more accuracy than my own. Knowing my inbuilt intolerance and an eagerness for Ben to do well, I'm guessing that rather than acting like a dad, I acted like a dick. At his first proper training session at his new club I had shown signs already of being the sporting parent that I knew I most definitely didn't want to be. I had become exasperated and critical of my own child simply because he didn't understand what was going on. I had been worried about what other children would think about him crying when of course they were all oblivious to him being upset because they were concentrating on what they themselves were doing. Also, a child crying is no big deal to other children because they all cry at some point. It is what they do! Looking deeper into it, I hadn't really been worried about what the other children would think, I had really been worried about what some of the other parents might think. Was I worrying that they would be judging my parenting skills?

'Look at that poor boy. His dad has brought him up so that he doesn't even understand tig, and rather than work it out he just burst into tears. Do we want him in our team?'

Some might have been thinking that. The majority probably weren't. Would I be judging another parent if their child was crying? Of course I wouldn't. But something strange happens to you when your child starts sporting activities. A pride overwhelms you.

You can fall into the trap of willing them to succeed in every drill, training session, game or race they participate in. Maybe doing it in a game of Crocodile is stretching it to the limit. You might start viewing them as an extension of yourself rather than the person they are in their own right. If they win that race or score that goal, are you as the parent taking some credit for passing on some of the genetics? Are you willing them to succeed so that they get all the attention and you can bask in the reflected glory? If they score a cracking goal, parents congratulate you often as much as they applaud your child. Or are you willing them to do well because maybe you didn't? You didn't win races or score amazing goals so this is the nearest thing you will ever come to that.

I had fallen into the trap within half an hour of watching Ben in action. I felt awful for the rest of that weekend and actually sitting here writing about how that morning panned out makes me feel terrible once more. I never wanted to get myself in that situation again. If I was ever going to get exasperated in the future, and it does happen from time to time, I would never ever show it outwardly. If any of the children do anything well in sport it is for them and them alone, not for me. I don't want the reflected glory of their achievements. I want them running races, scoring goals, swimming lengths and balancing on beams because they want to, because it makes them smile, not because I didn't or couldn't. One game of tig had done us all a favour but I also wonder that if Jessie had been the first-born, if Jessie had been playing Crocodile and had become confused and tearful, would I have been as frustrated? In simple terms, do I treat my son and daughter differently when it comes to sport?

Chapter 6

Jessie had been dragged round fields and halls within weeks of being born. Neither her mum nor her dad wanted to miss her brother's sporting activities so that meant she had to come too, whatever the weather. Being born in November she spent every weekend of those early months bundled up in her pram. A mass of blankets, romper suits, hats and mittens working as a barrier against the wind and the rain and on occasion the snow. A pink, runny nose often the only thing visible in among the synthetic fibres. The pram became a buggy, my baby daughter became a toddler but the blankets and the coats and the hats and the mittens remained. As did the pink, runny nose. Jessie never complained. This was just what we did on weekend mornings, it had become a way of life.

There would be other siblings dragged along to the park to watch the boys, many younger and of a similar age to Jessie, the odd older one with nothing else to do on a Saturday morning but not old enough to be left sleeping in their pit until mid afternoon. As they started to toddle and become more mobile they started to run around, often under the supervision of one of the older brothers or sisters. They were typical toddlers, curious, cheeky, always on the go. They wanted to play with everything they could see around them; balls, poles, cones, squirrels were all chased or run around. As every parent knows, you take your eyes off them at your peril. On several occasions I would take my phone out of my pocket, check my messages and then look up to see my daughter blissfully stumbling across a pitch towards the goal with twelve boys bearing down on her. They were oblivious to the intruder and only concentrating on getting to the ball. The boys would never stop, why would they? Scoring a goal and knocking over a small girl in the process, or picking up the ball and stopping the game to allow her to get off the pitch in safety? There is only one choice for a small boy. He would never stop. My daughter would be blissfully unaware of the danger heading her way. So that always meant I had to lumber across the field, often while still holding one of those polystyrene cups of coffee. I had to avoid the boys, try not to spoil the game, reach my daughter, scoop her up and try not to spill my drink. This wasn't too difficult, admittedly, but the problem was we now had a game, and I'm not talking about the football. I'm talking about Jessie thinking we had a game of chase going on. Once she was up and running, those Saturday mornings were as much about chasing her around and trying to stop her going on to the pitch as they were about watching Ben. She was also impossible to distract. A bottle of milk, a biscuit, a passing dog to pat and stroke, none of those things were as much fun as being chased by Daddy. Walk by any game of youth football on a weekend and I guarantee you will see at least one parent preoccupied with stopping a young child getting on to the pitch.

The constant exposure to the sport every weekend had obviously piqued her interest, added to the fact that she was regularly being clattered by her brother in the garden and having footballs fired at her head. If sport was playing such a large part in our family life, and it was, then she wasn't going to be left out and equally we didn't want her to be left out. So when Jessie said she wanted to play football properly, we had a responsibility to make sure she had the same opportunities as her brother. It was time for Little Kickers once again.

We had moved north so we were in a different venue, a school gym this time rather than a village hall. A polished floor, wooden bars attached to three of the room's four walls and benches either for the parents to sit on or for the kids to use to kick the balls against. Those benches haven't changed in design over the last forty years. The first tactic I had to learn at these sessions was not to get there late, otherwise I would have to sit right on the end of one of the benches where they have those two nobbly bits of wood for seemingly no reason at all except to make it rather uncomfortable on your backside.

Jessie was adamant she wanted to go in full kit for her first session. I can't remember what Ben wore for his first one, but Jessie had the full kit – shirt, shorts and socks pulled up to her knees. Not over her knees though, I wasn't having her imitate John Terry at her first football session. We arrived slightly early on the Sunday morning, so were encouraged by the organisers to grab a ball and start running around. Standing about waiting for others to arrive was not an option. So off this small bundle of energy ran to get a ball and then there I was playing football with my daughter, warming her up before she went through her first training routine. We passed the ball to each other, she scored several goals against one of the benches and generally ran around a lot. By the time everybody else arrived, her cheeks were flushed and her blonde hair was already trying to break free from the bobble keeping it in a ponytail. Also by the time everybody else arrived, she was the only girl there.

The session took me back just a few years to that village hall with Ben. Similar skills, similar routines, a similar sense of fun and joy and chaos with children and balls going in all directions around the room. I'd see my daughter miss balls, kick balls, score goals, fall over, bump into people, stop balls and run races. And after every single thing she did, good or bad, she would look over at me with a massive grin on her face. And I would grin back. I never felt exasperated, I never felt disappointed when she didn't get something right. I just felt happy that she was happy. My chest was bursting with pride. It is difficult to put into words the reason for such pride, which isn't particularly helpful when writing a book, but I will do my best.

I think it stemmed from the fact that she never once looked bothered about what anybody thought of her. If she didn't do something right, it didn't bother her. If she missed a ball or let a ball into the net or fell over then so what, she was just having fun. I think Ben felt like that in the early sessions too, so was there something else that was giving me this inordinate sense of pride? I have thought about it a lot and I think it also came from the fact that she was the only girl and most importantly she didn't care about it or maybe at such a young age didn't even notice that she was the only girl. This was something she wanted to do and she was going to do it. It most definitely wasn't about proving something to the boys – they were all too young to view anything as a battle of the sexes. It was about inclusion and through her enthusiasm and determination she had been included in a group of boys playing football. Of course Ben has been included in all his groups of boys who have played football over the years and

I feel pride at that, but he has never been different, he has never been the odd one out.

I felt nervous before those first few sessions, nervous on my daughter's behalf. Not nervous about her ability or whether she would be any good but nervous over her acceptance into the group. Nervous that she would be singled out or made to feel different because she was the only girl, but she never was so my nerves weren't necessary and disappeared after a couple of weeks. However, after a couple of months she decided she didn't want to keep the football going. Like so many children she was influenced by what her little friends were doing. Those nerves that had slipped away were going to come back with a vengeance and this time I would be nervous for myself, not for her, because I was about to enter a world I knew nothing about. A world I had never experienced before in my life. Jessie had decided she was going to try gymnastics.

With football I had known where to start with the children. In fact, with all the sports they have been interested in and wanted to try I have had some previous experience myself. From swimming to cricket, football to tennis I had tried them all and knew where to begin in getting my own kids on the ladder. With gymnastics, I had no clue whatsoever. So I did what I always do in situations where I feel helpless and clueless: I let my wife try to sort it out. Do you start at the local leisure centre? Are there gymnastics clubs that you can join? Do you just buy one of those ubiquitous middle-class trampolines for the garden and take it from there? All questions I couldn't answer, so it was down to Sara to hit the phones and the internet because I didn't want to look like an ignorant idiot. It turned out the answer to all three of the above questions was yes, so before I knew it we were heading to the leisure centre, investigating gym clubs in the area and spending several hours trying to put up a complicated piece of sporting equipment in the backyard. The first two combined took less time than the last one.

We were told, or rather Sara was told (I must stop the pretence here that this was a joint effort), that the leisure centre would be the best place to start. So for a couple of weeks we headed down as a family on a Friday afternoon to trampolining class. Class might be stretching it. For an hour we would go down and watch our child have three or four turns at bouncing up and down on a trampoline. Ben would come too and show absolutely no interest in watching his sister's efforts. Part of me would want to admonish him for his lack of interest. Jessie after all had come out in rain or shine – well, in rain or rain – to watch him do his early football, so the least he could do was reciprocate her support. Equally, I did share his lack of enthusiasm for watching a small child bounce for five minutes and couldn't blame him for wanting to kick anything he could deem ball-like up and down the corridor for the full sixty minutes. I showed great self-restraint and didn't join in with his football and instead stood on the balcony grinning and full of encouragement as I watched my daughter go up and down, up and down, up and down. I couldn't muster quite as much enthusiasm when the other children had their turns. It was one thing feigning interest when my own child was doing something not particularly interesting, but I would need Oscar-winning acting abilities to do it when it was somebody else's. My saving grace was that at least I was on the balcony shift. One adult with each child had to stand by the trampoline so Sara, along with other mums or dads, was in position by the equipment. They were like an England slip cordon, ready to catch an errant child who had got their bearings all wrong. It was a position of responsibility where you couldn't be distracted, hence why I was on the balcony. I didn't want to be the one checking my phone like I used to do at the football to suddenly find little Jonny rocketing over my head.

Jessie loved it and unlike with the earlier football she didn't want to stop, she wanted to do more. She was bouncing at the leisure centre and she was bouncing at home on her trampoline. She was full of laughter and giggles, me watching, petrified that I hadn't used the Allen key properly and that something was loose and that very shortly she wouldn't be bouncing any more, she would be on the back seat of my car on the way to A&E. Fortunately we never ended up in hospital thanks to my DIY incompetence, but we did eventually end up at weekly sessions at a local gymnastic club.

Sara had done all the research, all the planning, all the investigating and eventually found the right place for Jessie. It had a good reputation and was not too far from where we lived. Off the two of them would go on a Friday evening for an hour-long session, incorporating a variety of gymnastic disciplines, leaving myself and Ben to our own devices. I had kept my distance when it came to the trampolining and I hadn't been to her first few gym sessions, but I knew I couldn't continue being left to my own devices. At some point I was going to have to take a giant step into the unknown, or rather a giant step into the local gymnastics club. It had nothing to do with not wanting to watch gymnastics or a dislike of gymnastics, although it wasn't a sport that had enthralled me up to this point. I was genuinely scared stiff of going into an environment that I knew nothing about. Can you watch? Where do you watch? Do you follow your child around as they go from floor to beam to vault? What do you talk about with other parents? Can you walk out and go to the loo when somebody is in the middle of a floor routine? Could I take a drink in? Was I allowed to keep my phone on? The questions kept coming in my mind and then went out of my mouth to an increasingly exasperated wife who couldn't understand my discomfort.

She hadn't grown up in a sporting family. Her family had a musical background. When I went round to her house I was tripping up over music stands, sheet music, trumpets and bassoons (no, me neither) rather than cricket balls, tennis racquets and carpet bowls. Since we had had children, for her every foray into a different sport had been a journey into the unknown, full of questions of etiquette and what rules we had to adhere to, most of which, I grudgingly admit, I answered with the odd huff and puff and an air of exasperation. Now I was in her situation and to her credit, because she is nowhere near as petty as me, she didn't use it as a chance for revenge. She tried to allay my fears (yes fears, I realise that I was only going to my daughter's gym class but I was scared) and answered all my questions calmly with no sign of a huff or a puff.

With the questions answered but the fears definitely not allayed, the two of us set off for Jessie's Friday night gym class. Ridiculously, I peppered my daughter with questions about what was going to happen in the same way I had been interrogating my wife. Unsurprisingly she wasn't that bothered about what my experiences were going to be but was more interested in telling me how much she liked doing somersaults and how difficult she found doing a handstand.

We parked the car and I gave her some change to go and get a ticket from the pay and display machine. One of my many questions had uncovered that she liked to go and put the money in the machine herself. She bounded over and moments later bounded back with the ticket. Having stuck that on to the windscreen we headed inside, her little hand in mine. We walked past the reception and up a couple of flights of stairs. There was a throng of parents and children outside the room. I started to hang back.

'We can just go in, Daddy.'

'Oh, I'm not sure sweetheart. It looks like these people are waiting. We'd better just stay here with them.'

'No, I can go in, I need to get changed and ready.'

'Really?'

'Really,' she told me adamantly.

It was my first test. I hadn't been warned that there would be people waiting outside the room. If we went in would we disturb a class? Would there be tuts as we barged people aside, with them thinking *what is this clown doing, can't he see we're all waiting?*' A dilemma that most parents will have been in is *'Does my five-year-old know better than me?'* I decided on this occasion she had to. She had been here before, she knew how it worked and if she said she could go in then I had to let her and more importantly for me I had to go in with her, holding her hand. As uncomfortable as this sounds, I wanted to make sure everybody knew that I was there as a parent of a child taking part in the class. I didn't want anybody thinking I had just wandered in off the street like some kind of pervert to watch a children's gym class. It was an utterly ridiculous thing to think in some ways, because I have never felt like that watching my kids do any other sport and yet in other ways the world we now live in and the way society behaves sometimes makes you feel under suspicion when you are a middle-aged man watching a children's sporting event.

My dad was once asked to stop taking photos of his own grandson playing football at one tournament we were at. He was left utterly bemused and utterly angry at the request. He couldn't understand why he couldn't take pictures of his own flesh and blood playing sport. We were told that cameras weren't allowed at the event but there was an official photographer going around all the games taking shots. If we wanted some photos of Ben, we just had to let the photographer know which one he was and he would take some pictures of him. We would then be able to buy them. BUY them. This has happened at every organised tournament we have been to in a variety of sports, whether it be football, cricket, gymnastics or swimming. All have professional, official photographers in attendance to take the photos of your children that you are not allowed to. And every time, at every event, we end up buying some snaps of our little darlings. I don't know how much we are helping child protection but we are certainly helping the profits of the photographic industry. Though of course, the major plus point of the professional photo is that at least our child is in shot and in focus. I have a feeling that if I was taking them our house would be full of blurred photos, or photos of the odd limb, as one of our children ran out of shot just as I was hitting the take button.

There were no official photographers as we walked into the room, with the preceding class just coming to an end. I held Jessie's hand tight and stayed very close to her. I couldn't have made it more obvious if I had walked in holding her above my head like some trophy, shouting 'this is my daughter, MY daughter and that is why I am here, to watch her, MY daughter, perform her gymnastics.'

Jessie knew where she was headed, once inside the room, and still holding her hand I was dragged along to the spare chair she had spotted. She started to take off her tracksuit, and with a melee in the doorway as one class left and the new one arrived I was just grateful to plonk myself down on the empty chair and hope to blend into the background and not be disturbed or spoken to for the next hour or so. She put me in charge of her discarded tracksuit and her water bottle. We don't go anywhere as a family without taking water bottles. Sporting activities, the cinema, the zoo, the shops, the kids always take a water bottle with them. They don't often bring them back. We probably go through twenty water bottles a year. They even take one each to school with them. Back in my day, schools had things called taps but I'm assuming, given my wife's insistence on water bottles, that taps have gone the same way as blackboards and free school milk.

So with her tracksuit and bright pink water bottle safely guarded by her dad, she skipped off to find her friends. In among the throng of children, I could make out the equipment they would be using over the next hour. In the far corner of the rectangular-shaped room were the asymmetric bars. Huge foam mats had been built up to narrow the gap to the higher bar to make it easier for the little ones to reach it. Moving down from the bars, there was a floor area for the children to practise some of their routines to music, in the form of a small portable stereo system plugged in next to the thin blue mats to provide the soundtracks. Down the middle of the room ran a track. This was being inflated to provide spring for the older kids practising jumps and flips and somersaults in the air. Alongside the track, there were more thin blue mats, placed end to end. They led to a small springboard and then three huge foam mats. To the left of the foam mats were two beams. One was at its normal height, the other raised slightly off the floor. Then nearest the door was the warm up/cool down area, depending on whether you were starting or finishing the class. It was an impressive set-up for the children, who at a rough guess ranged from four all the way up to eleven or twelve. Stationed near each piece of apparatus were at least two older girls, wearing the club's shirts. They were clearly club gymnasts

themselves who were giving something back to the next generation. And they had to work very hard.

I didn't see everything that happened over the next two hours,
not for once because I became distracted and started playing on
my phone, but because the chair I was sitting on was behind the
large foam mats by the springboard and therefore my view of a
lot of things was obscured. If I had been feeling braver I would
have either moved my chair or moved myself, but I was so scared
of being shouted at that I just stayed where I was and relied on
fidgeting and craning my neck. A periscope would have been very
useful.

Just like with the trampolining, there were huge swathes of
time where my daughter was doing nothing bar talking to other
girls in the class. She had to wait her turn but when it was her
turn I had to make sure I was watching everything she did because once she finished she was looking over for approval.

One of the girls lifted her on to the asymmetric bars and her
little hands gripped on for dear life. And she just hung there.
For ten seconds. And was then lifted off. Her eyes immediately
searched for me and when they locked on I gave her a big thumbs
up. For holding on for ten seconds. She took two steps on the
lower beam and looked over at me. And fell off. I silently applauded her and she beamed, pun intended. She would take a big
run at the springboard and then as she reached it, she would stop
dead. Then she jumped on to it, with no momentum whatsoever,
and had to clamber on to the foam mats. Another big thumbs up
from her daddy. On the floor exercises she would try to do those
handstands she found so difficult, but she had no strength in those
little arms so she needed to be helped by her coaches. She could,
though, forward roll to her heart's content. She would do five or
six and then rush over to me purple-faced and smiling for a cuddle

and a drink from the water bottle. I had no idea whether she was good or bad, if she was doing things correctly or not, but the only thing that mattered was she was happy. Actually that's not strictly true. It wasn't the only thing that mattered. It also mattered that I had got through the session without being in the wrong place at the wrong time or being shouted at. I had come through the experience unscathed.

At bang on eight o'clock the class came to an end. The gymnasts were asked to line up in the warm-down area in height order. At ten past eight they had just about sorted themselves out after disagreements over whether somebody's bun made them taller than a girl with just a simple ponytail. With Jessie at the smaller end of the line, they all then had to 'present' to the head coach before they could leave. This involved the line, as a whole, taking one step forward with bent knee and putting both arms up in the air and saying 'thank you coach' in response to the coach's 'thank you gymnasts'. I found it quite a nice, polite way to end the session, certainly compared to a football training session where everybody tends to slope off at the end.

Back in the car, and with tracksuit on but water bottle left in the gymnastics room, Jessie enthused about the previous couple of hours. She barely paused for breath. She had loved this and loved that and was delighted she could do a forward roll.

'Can you do a forward roll, Daddy?'

'Of course, Jessie. I can even do a backward roll.'

'What about a handstand?' she enquired, having struggled with this herself during the session.

I had already been economical with the truth when I threw the backward roll into the conversation. If I said yes here it would be a blatant lie.

'Yes.'

'Could you show me when we get home?'

Oh shit, shit shit. I needed to qualify this somehow.

'Well, when I said yes, Jessie, what I meant was I used to be able to do a handstand but as I've got older and bigger I have found it harder, so it might be a bit difficult for me to show you when we get home,' I said, feeling a mixture of pride that I had come up with a plausible excuse and shame that I had lied about it in the first place.

'Well could you at least try? Please?' – and she gave me that look that all fathers will recognise from their daughters. That look that it is impossible to say no to. A look that will never change as she progresses into being a teenager and then into adulthood.

We arrived home. Jessie bounced through the front door, ironically with more bounce than when she hit the springboard in the class, and if you think I am being unduly harsh on my small daughter here then don't forget that she is going to make me try to do a handstand in just a few moments' time.

'Daddy is going to show me how to do a handstand,' she announced to the household as we went into the lounge. Laughter seemed to echo around the house as both my wife and my son sprinted to join us.

'Really?' said my wife, biting down on her lip.

'Yes, really,' replied my daughter with apparent innocence, although I remain convinced that even at such a young age she knew what she was doing.

I positioned myself in such a way that if this went disastrously wrong I wouldn't crash into the television but might clout my son in an act of retribution for laughing so much. I put my hands on the floor, bent over and tried to lift my legs up. I could barely lift them more than six inches off the floor.

'I did say, Jessie, it gets harder as you get older,' I grimaced, as laughter burst out again. 'Plus sweetheart, it is very difficult to do, so your attempts at it were very good and much better than mine.' I thought praise might distract her and that we could end this here and I could go and get a beer from the fridge.

'Give it one more go.' She wasn't distracted.

The second time was no better and no worse than the first time. Hands on the floor, legs bent and six inches off the ground.

'Do a somersault then,' she implored. 'You said you could do one of them.'

'OK. One forward roll coming up and then I need a beer.' I knew I could do this. It would all be over very quickly.

'Here we go then.' Into position I crouched. 'One, two, three', and over I went in a cacophony of thuds, creaks and cracks. The thuds came from the floorboards, even though they were cushioned by the carpet. The creaks and cracks came from my spine, neck and shoulders. I lay there moaning and groaning, the three other members of the family looking over me, laughing.

I wasn't seriously hurt of course, just a bit sore and slightly humiliated. I was a sportsman. I had run and swum and scored goals and made tackles and won headers. I'd taken wickets, hit a boundary and won tennis matches. I had even broken ninety at golf and yet here I was flat on my back and being laughed at by my loved ones after one somersault. Where had it gone wrong? Of course, really, looking back at my sporting life, the question should have been . . .

When had it ever been right?

Chapter 7

They put me in goal. They put me IN GOAL. I was so happy. I would have things to do and I could use my hands and I would have to save my team and I'd get a different coloured shirt and I could be a hero. A hero! Along with the striker for the Cubs' football team, all eyes would be on me. The attention always goes to the one who puts the ball in the net and the one who keeps it out. And it wasn't just the coach of the Cubs' football team who had spotted my goalkeeping talent; the teacher at my primary school was also short of volunteers to go in goal so had chosen me to be the goalkeeper for his side as well. The opportunity for some heroic goalkeeping for two teams; perfect!

Once I knew I was going to be a goalkeeper for two sides, I had to set about getting the right kit. I did this by nagging my parents until they gave in, a method that seems to have been passed down through generations of Chapmans; all my children seem to possess this gene and exhibit it on what feels like a weekly basis. They, of course, are asking for a lot more, a lot more frequently, than I ever did. I had a pair of boots so all I needed were some gloves and a goalkeeper's shirt. The shirt was just a standard green jersey with a black trim running from the shoulder all the way down the arm to the cuff on both sides.

The gloves were a sight to behold. Nowadays a huge amount of science goes into sportswear and goalkeepers' gloves are no different. A press release normally accompanies each new design stating that they have been tested in outer space and are the most complete (insert type of sportswear) ever made. They will absorb / release heat (delete as applicable) and have been tested in the hottest / coldest (again delete as applicable) environments known to man. They are designed for the modern sporting individual and will make you run faster, catch better, pass more accurately, throw further and be the most amazing sportsperson the world has ever seen! That said, at the same time said product has been designed with a nod to history and to take into account the heritage of whatever sport you are competing in. If Joe Hart was to wear gloves that had taken into account a nod to history by incorporating a design similar to the ones I had worn, he would run out for England looking like he was about to do an afternoon's gardening.

My gloves were made of a red cloth material. Stuck on to each finger, the thumb and the palm area of the glove were strips of pimples made of some rubber-like material. These strips appeared to be of random size and didn't cover the whole of the areas they were attached to. Most of them came about halfway down each finger, thereby covering each tip and maybe about two-thirds of the palm. I am assuming, because this agricultural piece of sporting equipment didn't come with a press release, that these pimple strips were designed to help you catch the ball. The confusing thing about these gloves was that the pimple strips were also attached to the back of the gloves as well, on each finger, the thumb and the back of the hand area. As I found out early on in my goalkeeping career, you shouldn't be trying to catch the ball with the back of your hand.

The bottom of each glove also had an elasticated strip with a Velcro fastener. This would cause me great discomfort because the Velcro fastener would always make one wrist or the other itch, and once it started to itch I needed to scratch it. But, of course, I couldn't scratch it properly because I had a glove on my other hand and the nail couldn't get through the cloth of the glove. So I would have to take that glove off so I could have a proper scratch of the wrist that was itching. I would then have one glove off and one glove on while having a good scratch, feeling that intense satisfaction and warmth one gets when relieving oneself of an itch – when the opposition came bearing down on my goal, clean through. The ball invariably was in the back of my net as I was still itching, scratching and trying to pull my glove back on with my teeth. I certainly wasn't looking heroic. I never looked heroic as a goalkeeper.

It is easy to blame your surroundings or your environment rather than your sheer lack of ability in these situations, but as any child of the 1980s will testify, playing kids' football in that decade was not easy. We did not have small-sided games, we did not play on smaller pitches and we did not have smaller goals. After an awful lot of soul searching and after an awful lot of early exits from European Championships and World Cups the foot-balling authorities in this country eventually got their act together and changed how our children play football. We were thirty years too early to benefit.

We would run ourselves to exhaustion, playing on full-size pitches. At the age of seven and eight the only way we could get the ball from one half to another, let alone from one end of the pitch to the other, was to give it to the biggest lad in the side and get him to hoof it as hard as he could. Keeping the ball and playing lovely passing football was not an option. Huge swathes of the pitch would not have a player in them, as most boys were drawn to the ball. Sixteen, eighteen maybe even twenty lads all trying to get the ball at the same time in one small area of grass with just the two goalkeepers in space. The two goalkeepers, of which I was one, looking tiny, standing in a full-size penalty area and of course guarding a full-size goal. Two Lilliputians watching on as twenty boys took ten minutes to release the ball from a melee of legs.

Ben never had this problem when he started playing matches. They were playing 7-a-side games on small pitches that were roughly the length of one half of a full-sized pitch, with two small goals at either end. The goalkeepers at that age couldn't reach the crossbar but at the same time wouldn't have needed to build a tower of teammates, shoulders on shoulders, to have touched it, which had been the case for me.

The size of the goal and the size of the pitch made my eighteen months of being a goalkeeper a miserable experience. On those rare occasions when I wasn't scratching and I had managed to keep both gloves on, I still wasn't keeping much out. Unless the ball came straight at me, there was very little I could do to prevent it going into the gargantuan net behind me. Shot after shot would fly over my head and into the middle of the goal. Even more humiliating than conceding the goals was when the opponent missed altogether, leaving me with a goal kick. This meant that I couldn't advance to the edge of my area and throw the ball out or kick it out from my hands; instead I had to place the ball on the corner of the six yard box and kick it off the ground with all the strength my little legs could muster. On a good day

I would manage to clear the penalty area. Yes, on a good day I would manage to kick that ball twelve yards or more. The rule in football is that from a goal kick the ball has to travel outside the penalty area for the game to continue. If it doesn't then the kick has to be retaken. There were some goal kicks that I had to retake four or five times and every time I had to retake them the opposition were encouraged to get nearer and nearer to our box, in the knowledge that the ball wasn't going to go very far. By the time I was on my third retake I would be looking up to see all twenty outfield players stood on the edge of our box, daring me to try to kick it over them. This wasn't, however, an experience unique to me. The opposition keeper would be going through something similar when the ball was at his end as well.

In a desperate attempt to try to discover some kind of enjoyment from playing in goal, I persuaded my parents to buy me a new goalkeeping jersey. I realise there is very little logic in that sentence but it seemed a vital necessity at the time. Every opposition keeper, whether I was playing for my school or the Cubs, wore green. I suppose the eighties were a very conservative time in all respects of the word. However I had seen a different coloured top in the local sport shop. My dad seemed to go to Cooper Sports a lot when I was growing up, mainly to buy squash equipment. In fact, mainly to buy squash balls as he seemed to lose an awful lot to the extractor fan that overlooked the main court at his club. I found it a magical place and could while away plenty of time marvelling at shiny sports equipment, the array of balls (not just squash ones) and various strips and kits. While he was digging out a couple of boxes of 'yellow spots', I started flicking through the rails. In among the Adidas Manchester United shirts and the Admiral England tops, I discovered a plain goalkeeping top. But not in green. In red. Using that persuasive, pleading tone of voice that winds me up so much nowadays when my own children use it, I managed to get my dad to throw the shirt in with his squash balls.

It had no effect, except to end my goalkeeping career. Not long into the life of the red goalkeeping top we came up against an opposition side who played in red. Nobody even passed comment about me clashing with them. The first time it came to anybody's attention was when one of our own players kicked me very hard, thinking I was on the other side. The opposition had had a corner. Via a couple of flick-ons it had eventually arrived in the box. It bounced and I decided I could catch it, although given the usual standard of my performances there was no guarantee I would. My teammate, seeing a flash of red, assumed it was an opposition player and went to clear the ball. My hand got to the ball first, his boot got to my arm, tears welled up in my eyes. As I crumpled on the floor, I heard the boy say he thought I was one of them, and with that comment light bulbs went on in everybody's head and they suddenly realised I was wearing the same colour top as the opposition. My dad came on to the pitch, carried me off and drove me home. I had a bruise on my arm and my mum wondered whether I should get it seen to, but my dad said it would be fine, particularly 'after a good night's sleep'. As I lay in bed, wondering how that could cure a potentially broken arm (it wasn't, but I've never been good with pain), I knew I didn't want to play in goal ever again.

My school immediately had a plan; they were going to play me left midfield. I couldn't kick with my left foot, I had no pace and I had no skills or tricks with which I could beat a man. If I didn't know better I would say that they were just trying to put me out of the way in a position where I could do very little damage to my own team. And there I stayed for the majority of my primary school career, marooned out on the left wing. From that period, though, I can remember the names of the schools we played against. I can remember the names of a lot of my team-mates, too. Barry Hope is the one that stands out more than most on account of the fact that he was the one who had been for a trial at Manchester City. I can remember the kits and the name of the teacher in charge but I can't remember a single thing I did to contribute to the Sandilands Junior School football team between the years of 1980 and 1984. I did play though and I do feature on all the team photos. Acrylic blue and white shirt and tight, very short shorts displaying stick-thin thighs and very white knees. On every team photo I had the appearance of someone who had performed a knee slide through a puddle of whitewash when in fact it was just a severe case of eczema. In my third year at junior school I was asked to stand on the teacher's desk at the front of the room so that the rest of the class could draw me for an art project. The results were variable at best and yet every single child, without exception, drew me with massive white patches on both knees. The playground chant, sung to the tune of the Cadbury's flake advert, was 'only the crumbliest, flakiest Chapman'. I was more known at the school for my knees than my football.

My time with the Cubs didn't last much longer and I joined a local football club, Brooklands Youth FC. Black and yellow striped shirts. Black shorts. Black socks. A lot of the Cubs' side joined too, so the most important thing for me to do at the start was to make everyone aware that playing goalkeeper or left wing were not my strong points and were two positions I had no inclination of revisiting. A group of dads were in charge of this side and they wanted to make sure their sons were in their favoured positions before everything else was divvied up. Centre forwards and centre midfielders were in abundance or maybe dads of centre forwards and centre midfielders were in abundance. We also had some quick and skilful players who could play out wide, so by a process of elimination I ended up as a centre half. As hopefully you will discover later on it is a position that has given me enormous pleasure over the years, but the way we arrived at it back then is indicative of how random and I suppose shambolic my early footballing years were compared to my son's.

Ben was starting even earlier than I had done. His crushing experience with the Crocodile game had come at a much younger age than my crushing goalkeeping experiences, closely followed by my crushing left wing experiences and rounded off by my crushing knee experiences. And yet even though he was starting at a younger age, everything seemed more structured and much better organised than it had been for me and my teammates.

Ben recovered well after struggling to understand the rules of a basic game of tig. Sorry, I had forgotten when I wrote that sentence that I am meant to be more sympathetic and understanding. Let's try again . . .

Ben recovered well after understandably becoming disorientated and confused and overwhelmed on his first day at the club by a complicated game with a frightening name and I could see his progression on a weekly basis.

The boys and girls were coached and cajoled for ninety minutes every Saturday morning and would then play small-sided games against each other. For an amateur club, completely self-funded with a shirt sponsorship deal from the Football Foundation, they did exceptionally well to provide all the equipment they did. Cones, bibs, poles, tiny goals only slightly bigger than an actual football and the larger goals for matches were all available as was, most importantly, a football for every single boy in the group. A complete contrast to my early days, where we had none of that and maybe two balls between our whole group. How can you develop as a footballer if you don't have a ball to work with when you practise? Ben continued to work on the skills he had tried to learn in his Little Kickers days and he was encouraged to do so by the coaches. If he wanted to try something he had seen Cristiano Ronaldo do then why not? If, in a similar situation, I had tried to recreate a little bit of Zico magic at the Cubs, I would have first fallen over in a failed heap and secondly I would have been discouraged from trying it again.

That said, I wouldn't have been exposed to very many tricks. The football we saw on the television constituted *Match of the Day* on the BBC and *The Big Match* on ITV. You occasionally saw some on a midweek *Sportsnight* or on your regional ITV station but that was it. There would be maybe two chances per week to watch football and only from English leagues. I don't think I had heard of La Liga or the Bundesliga until I was in my teens. Ben would see skills from across the globe on a daily basis and would want to try them out straight away. He'd be able to see a skill, record it, pause it and watch how it was done, or call it up on YouTube and take it out into the garden with him and practise and practise and practise. He would then be able to try it with his mates at the Saturday training and similarly his mates would be bringing different skills that they had seen for him to try. Positions didn't matter, how to play in an actual game didn't matter – one of the few similarities with my era was that when they played a game they all flocked to the ball, well, like bees around a honeypot – the score of the games didn't matter. As twee as it sounds, just like Little Kickers before, the only thing that mattered was that they were enjoying themselves.

The children had a good eighteen months in this regular pattern; good coaching, good fun and with a real noticeable improvement in their abilities. As they reached their last couple of months in this group, the summer months of 2009, things began to change. Things started to become more structured. When September came around the children would start to play games against other clubs in the area, so they needed to be prepared for this. The games wouldn't be competitive, in the sense that there wouldn't be points awarded for a win or a draw and there wouldn't be a league table so nobody could finish top or bottom.

The theory behind that reasoning is that by doing away with points and a league table, the whole thing should be more harmonious for everybody concerned. If you take out the 'win at all costs' mentality, the kids should enjoy it more and the weaker sides in particular would not feel humiliated by constantly looking at a league table and seeing themselves near or on the bottom. The coaches' modus operandi should be about improving each individual in their charge and not about setting up the side to win every game, which at that age is simply about getting the ball to the biggest/quickest/most skilful lad and letting him do the rest. Without points being at stake, the referees should be able to use their own discretion and common sense. The children are too young to understand all the rules so they shouldn't be refereed as if they are in a World Cup final. Leniency should be encouraged. The final part of that theory is that the parents should be able to watch with a smile on their faces, with plenty of encouragement in their voices and with appreciation for every single player on that pitch, whether good or bad, in your own team or in the opposition's.

That's the theory.

Chapter 8

There was competition in the air before they had even played a game. Those summer months were filled with nudges and gossip and a lot of dads telling their kids what to do. A side was weeks away from being formed and every parent wanted to make sure their child was in it. Each training session was bookended with besieged coaches being asked by parents how their child was doing.

'What could he improve on?'

'Everything, he's only six.'

'Where is he going to play?'

'He'll play everywhere, because he's only six and they tend to just run around a lot at this stage.'

'Is it worth giving him extra coaching?'

'Just kick a ball with him in the garden.'

'He can't wait to start the matches and get stuck in.' (Desperately trying to find out if he was going to be selected in a less than subtle way.)

'Well the games are still weeks off so there's no point worrying about that just yet.' (Realising easily what the parent was trying to find out and playing it back with a straight bat, if you can play a straight bat to a footballing question.)

As I am lucky enough in my job to be surrounded by professional sports people who quite often rant about the state of children's sport and the behaviour of some parents in particular – yes, Chris Waddle, I am talking about you here – I was adamant I wasn't going to be one of those parents. Plus I had Sara bringing up the Crocodile experience on a regular basis to keep me in check, so I just observed these conversations and tried to stay out of it. At the same time I was itching to ask similar questions about Ben.

Is he good enough? Is he among the best fifteen or so players in his age group at the club? What could he improve on? Is he running enough? He doesn't look like he's involved a lot sometimes. Why is that? Why did you put him in goal in that session? He was off the field for ten minutes during that small-sided game. Why? Why are you playing him in that position? That doesn't help him. Are you going to pick him? ARE YOU GOING TO PICK HIM?

Not once did I ask the coaches any of those questions. I knew it wouldn't do Ben, me or them any good. But I couldn't keep the questions in my head. They would be going around and around and causing me great turmoil, so I needed to get them out somehow. I needed to be reassured that my son would be OK and would be part of the team. So instead of talking to somebody at the club, I would put the questions to my wife.

My wife, who had no background in football, who wouldn't know whether someone was playing well or badly or even at that stage what the difference was between a corner and goal kick, was the one I would seek reassurance from about our son's footballing ability. Ridiculously and embarrassingly, it would dominate so many conversations. Car journeys, walks back home having dropped him at school, even the odd romantic dinner, would all at some point include a 'Do you think he's going to get in?' followed by a huge sigh from across the table or the passenger seat.

'I have no idea. Once again, you know more about this than me.'

'Yes, but have you heard anything? Have any of the mums said anything? Have any of the boys said anything to the mums who have then said something to you? Or have any of the boys said anything to the mums who have then said something to each other that you have then overheard because you are very good at earwigging?'

An argument would then follow about whether she was or wasn't good at listening in to other people's conversations and how much of a gossip she was or wasn't, before we would then get back round to Ben's chances.

'So I have no idea,' she would reiterate, 'what do you think?'

'Well . . .' At which point I would spend ten minutes tying myself in knots over the positives and negatives of Ben's performances at football training and we would be spending the large part of a romantic dinner for two discussing the footballing abilities of our six-year-old and for that matter other six-year-olds in his group as we compared them.

'Do you think we should move him?' was the question I would ask more often than not to round the conversation off.

'Move him?' This was followed by another exasperated sigh, as she geared up for her final point which would bring it to an end. For now. 'He's happy, he's with his mates, the coaches are great so why move him? Where would he go?'

'You're right. I know. You're right. He's happy and with his friends and that's all that matters. Shall we get the bill?'

As I used one hand to motion a pen while using my left hand to represent a piece of paper, she knew, and I knew that she knew, that even though I knew he was happy and with his friends and that our discussion had now ended for this evening, in my head I was thinking, *'If he can just improve his tackling he'll definitely make the side.'*

Love was rarely, if ever, in the air that summer.

Ben was utterly oblivious to my turmoil, which is the way it should be, and of course my turmoil was a complete waste of time because by the time September came around he was in the squad with all of his friends. In fact they all were because at that age there is more than enough football to go around, whatever the ability of the child. People aren't available every week, you can have lots of substitutes and with all amateur football, from Under-7s all the way up to veterans, sometimes people just don't turn up. There would be plenty of games for Ben and his friends.

Two coaches had been put in charge of this squad. Their main coach was a sixteen-year-old girl who was playing football at a decent standard herself, and her dad would help her out as someone who had been at the club for several years. She would take the training and coach them during the games, he would help with the logistical side of things and referee the home games. He had also been there and done it all before so when there were issues, as there were bound to be, he would be on hand to smooth things over. An experienced parent would have problems from time to time with a group of six-year-old boys, let alone a teenager.

The training continued as before, on a Saturday morning, and games against other local sides were arranged for the Sunday mornings. Early starts both weekend mornings then. Great. The parental sacrifices for children to do their sport had begun and they were only ever going to increase. Dealing with the early starts and dealing with all those other sacrifices you make along the way are easy compared to trying to deal with the nerves. Not dealing with the nerves of your children before they swim, run, hit or kick, it's dealing with your own nerves that's the problem.

The morning of his first game, I felt sick. I needn't have worried about dealing with an early start because I had been tossing and turning most of the night, so when daylight came it was actually a relief to get out of bed. A sleep-deprived night all because of an Under-7s game of football. Ben had slept just fine in case you were wondering. He was a bundle of energy through breakfast and through getting ready. I was quiet and alone with my thoughts and my thoughts this time, I believe, were understandable, not ridiculous like they had been earlier on in the summer.

My overriding thought was simply: *'I hope he'll be OK.'*

I wanted this amazing little person that we are bringing up and who is so full of enthusiasm and energy to enjoy the morning. I wanted his first-ever game for the club to make his eyes sparkle, his cheeks flush and his mouth grin. Hand on heart I can say that I didn't care whether his team won or lost. I didn't care whether he scored a goal or seven or whether he set up a goal or seven. I just wanted him to be happy and if he could avoid dropping a massive bollock in the process that would be great too.

Ben's team were at home, so once we pulled into the car park he was out of the door and running off to join his teammates, confident he knew where he was going and desperate to get away from his unusually contemplative father. I ambled along behind him, still turning things over in my mind, and was greeted by a group of the other dads. There were mumbles and handshakes and occasionally someone would try to start a discussion about the professional games of football that had taken place the day before, but it felt like nobody was in the mood for conversation and most eyes were on the boys as they tore around the park. It was inevitable that before long one dad told his son to calm down and save his energy for the big game coming up, forgetting both that it wasn't a big game, just a friendly, and that six-year-olds have enough energy to run around for hours on end.

Our low-hum group mumbling session was interrupted by a call to arms from our father and daughter coaching duo. If we had raised our heads to look out across the park we would have noticed that there was no pitch set up. There were several that had been marked with the correct whitewashed lines but there was an absence of goals and corner flags. We were told that one of the important roles of the home team's parents was to get the pitch ready, so could we crack on with it, please? Four corner flags could be found just inside the store cupboard on the left-hand side of the clubhouse, and also in there could be found two large bags with the goals in them. Excuse us. The goals were in bags? They weren't in the yard, round the back, just waiting to be dragged out? Oh no, these goals needed building.

The group immediately split into two: those who saw the idea of building two small goals for the children as no big deal and others whose faces immediately gave the impression that they had been asked to build the Eiffel Tower out of matchsticks in just twenty minutes. Given it once took me over four hours to build a futon from IKEA you can easily deduce which group I fell into. I made a dart for the store cupboard and grabbed the corner flags.

As I walked round the pitch planting the corner flags and two groups of dads wrestled with plastic tubes, nets, hooks and pegs, the boys started to warm up with their coaches. Could the dads get the goals ready before the kids were ready to go? Just. As I had been cowardly enough to choose the corner flag task, I was assigned another job before I could grab a coffee and endure – sorry, enjoy – the actual football. I had to put out the barrier. Yes, there is now a barrier at every children's football match, to keep the parents at a safe distance from their own offspring!

I was directed to another bag in the store cupboard and with it slung over my shoulder I headed back towards the pitch. On opening the bag I discovered approximately twenty vibrantly orange plastic posts. These had to be planted at equidistant intervals along one of the touchlines. To go with the building challenge of the goals, there was now a mathematical puzzle as well. If I put the posts too close together I wouldn't have enough of them for the whole touchline, if they were too far apart the tape I had to loop through each one wouldn't be taut enough. It was a lot to deal with on a Sunday morning, with my son about to play his first proper match. Fortunately, a couple of other parents decided not to leave me up to my own devices and helped and quite quickly the posts were out and the blue and white tape, emblazoned with the Football Association logo and the word Respect, was successfully looped through. We had positioned the barrier five yards away from the pitch and all parents and spectators had to remain behind it throughout. On no account were we to stand behind either goal, now fully assembled (yay, go dads), and the far side of the pitch was reserved for the coaches and the substitutes, so that was out of bounds too.

Depending on your own sporting experiences, as either a player or a parent, it may seem extreme to have to put up tape to give the children some space away from the spectators, but it is a decent idea. On the odd occasions I have been at a game where the tape isn't there, parents automatically stand right on the touchline. If Philip Larkin had written about your mum and dad at a football match he would have still been right to suggest 'they fuck you up', but he could well have added 'and they generally just get in the way'. Without that tape they just nudge forward and nudge forward until they are actually standing on the pitch, trying to peer around whoever is standing next to them to get a view of their own little angel. Dads, with a combination of over-eagerness and a desperation to show anyone there that they can play themselves, try to control the ball as it is going out for a throw-in, but often don't wait for it to actually cross the line, thereby causing exasperation from the referee, tuts from other parents and bemusement from the children who are still trying to learn the rules. It can be chaotic. The tape really does stop that and of course it is also there to stop angry parents from running on to the field of play to confront the referee, the opposition or even their own child, though in reality it wouldn't be too hard to jump over a two-foot-high piece of tape.

What the tape cannot stop is sound and within minutes of the boys kicking off in their first ever game against another team, they were exposed to a barrage of noise.

'Kick it!'

'Pass it!'

'Tackle!'

'Run!'

'Mark!'

'Shoot!'

'Get rid!'

'Clear it!'

'Catch it!'

'Move!'

'Stay!'

'No, definitely move!'

'No, definitely stay!'

'Use your head!'

'Stay calm!' (the irony)

'Find a teammate!'

'Stop biting your nails!' (that was us because Ben constantly had his fingers in his mouth)

'Concentrate!'

'Well done!'

'Keep going!'

'Take the throw!'

'Take the corner!'

'Take the goal kick!'

'Kick it harder!'

'No, kick the ball, not that little boy!'

'Get it wide!'

'Get it forward!'

'Get it anywhere!'

'Get it in the goal!'

Both sets of supporters were getting rid of more nervous energy than the actual players by creating a cacophony of nonsensical bollocks. There was so much confusion that the boys understandably didn't know whether they were coming or going. It was draining for all concerned.

Maybe it says something about that first game that I can't actually remember whether Ben's team won or lost, but I can remember the pre-game tasks and the parental behaviour. No matter what sport your child does, it wouldn't happen without parents giving up their time to help their children and ferry them around. Yes, they might shout nonsense but the majority are doing it with the best of intentions. It also wouldn't happen without the thousands of volunteers who give up their time on a daily or weekly basis to help other people's kids have fun and reach their potential. They encourage, they cajole, they advise, often simply because they want to give something back to the sport they love.

Equally – from swimming to tennis, football to gymnastics, cricket to netball – I have spoken to numerous coaches who are frustrated at having to spend as much time firefighting and dealing with uninterested children as they do coaching and helping the ones who want to be there. The cost of childcare escalates by the year and parents have to work, they can't take every school holiday off, unless they are teachers, but it helps nobody, least of all their own child, to put them into an activity they don't want to do. They wouldn't leave them on an Outward Bound course every day for a week: 'Here you are darling, I know you have no interest in this but you are going to spend the week abseiling because I can't sort out childcare.' They wouldn't put them in a music group: 'I know you have never done this before sweetheart, but just play with this French horn for a week and join in with all the other kids while I go to work.' I am not sure the organisers would allow it either. Health and safety would probably rule out the abseiling for a start while the music teacher wouldn't allow their orchestra to be disrupted by little Jonny randomly blowing on a French horn for five hours a day. Yet, we seem to accept it when it comes to sport. What harm can be done? If the child doesn't like football then he can just mess around and it will be fine. Well it won't be.

A coach has to be taken away from what they are meant to be doing to try to make the uninterested interested. It distracts the children who do want to be doing their sport by both disrupting the game they are playing and also planting the seed in their heads that they can mess about too. It also creates a miserable experience for the child in question. They don't want to be there, they are there through no fault of their own and they find themselves being coerced into doing something they don't want to do. Parents shouldn't force their children to do sport and shouldn't look on sport as a get-out to help them with their own busy lives.

On top of which, coaches not only have to deal with the children in their charge, but they also have to deal with being scrutinised every step of the way by the parents. Parents who more often than not think that they know better. Parents who think they know better but won't actually volunteer to help out. Having experienced that scrutiny, I always try now to drop my kids off with their coaches and then keep my distance and let them get on with it. Once I've checked I haven't put them in the hands of a madman, obviously. I do have some sense of parental responsibility.

Chapter 9

Mr Greene was in charge of the school team at Sandilands, the man who put me in goal. At secondary school, Mr Moss, Mr Hardiman, Mr Hearne, Mr Brierley and Mr Edwards guided me through the ups and downs of my teenage football. Mr Edwards, in particular, I retain a soft spot for because he managed me for a couple of years compared to just one with all the others, plus he seemed to delight in my uncouth, agricultural, slightly cumbersome approach to the game and didn't try to change me. Breaking it down, I liked him because he had no problem with me hoofing it fifty yards and didn't try to force me to play short five-yard passes to my fullbacks or into midfield.

I remember them all because they each played a part in my growth as a player, both literally and metaphorically. Even though they were all teachers and were therefore paid to look after me during the day, they all gave up their time to allow us pupils to train and play football. However, there is still a teacher–pupil relationship there at all times and all of the above men were still referred to as 'sir', both at training and on match day. So even though I am grateful for all they did for me as their combination guided me from eight to seventeen years of age, I reserve most of my affection for a man who took charge of my club side, Brooklands Youth FC, for several years. The one and only Dick Crotty.

I tell my children that during their sporting childhood there will be one coach who they will remember way into adulthood; when they are in the park with their own kids or when they are standing at the side of a game or a race they will look back and still see that coach clearly at the forefront of their mind. For me, Dick Crotty is that man.

He sounds like a character out of a Harry Potter novel but he was a kind, enthusiastic man full of love for the game and a willingness for us, as a group, to improve and enjoy our football. There were never ever any histrionics from the sideline from him and we respected him. We respected him so much that we never called him Dick, it was always Mr Crotty. He was a thin, fit man, with soft brown eyes. His crown was bald but he had tufts of black hair with flecks of grey on each side of his head and around the back. There may well have been the odd tuft coming out of his ears and his nose; it happens to us all in middle age. I assumed he was in his late fifties or sixties but in a recent conversation with my mum she thought he was younger than that, probably in his forties, and that I was just suffering from the belief that all children suffer from, that most adults they come into contact with are just really, really ancient. I am ashamed to say that when I left Brooklands I don't remember saying a proper thank you to him. I would love to have that opportunity even now, but I am also ashamed to say that I have no idea whether he is still alive.

Why would I want to thank him? I think in the main because he kept my enthusiasm for football up through those difficult teenage years. Maybe I am so sport obsessed that my enthusiasm would have stayed regardless, but with my son just entering his teens I am witnessing first-hand how easy it is for some of them to start to drift away. All of a sudden, to a lot of them staying in bed seems preferable to getting up on a cold Sunday morning. Staying up until midnight to watch something on television or even go out with a girl is a lot more fun than an early night to make sure they are ready for a match. There is also less acceptance of a substitute role. If they are going to be getting up early and are cold they want to play, not stand on the touchline.

I never felt like this while playing for Mr Crotty, although it probably helped that I didn't discover girls until I was much older. I never wanted to miss a game, I never wanted to miss training and over the years our team hardly changed. A few players joined but hardly any fell by the wayside, one or two at most, hence I could name so many of my teammates earlier on in the book. We were a well-drilled, close-knit bunch. We won many more games than we lost and on occasion even found ourselves close to success with the odd battle for a league title. Note I didn't say we won a league title: there is a distinct absence of trophies and medals in this book, unless I can squeeze in later how I came to win 'Cub of the Month'.

Each season passed under the watchful eye of Mr Crotty. Win, lose or draw there was never any shouting from him – there was from some of the dads, but not from him. As twee as it sounds, as long as we did our best he was happy. But we had to be dressed correctly. If we weren't, we were in trouble. Mr Crotty had one strict rule on match day, and this is an example of what I mean when I say that the coach one has at a young age can still be an influence many, many years later. He didn't like us wearing anything under our team shirts, and to this day I still feel like I am betraying the Mr Crotty ethos if I wear an extra layer.

Our strip was a black and yellow striped shirt with black shorts and black socks. The shirt had a V-neck collar that while not plunging, it was a child's football shirt after all, certainly wasn't tight to the neck. If on a cold day a player had put a T-shirt on underneath the black and yellow stripes then the top of the T-shirt would be visible to all. Mr Crotty wouldn't allow this. He thought it looked scruffy first and foremost and he also thought that if a couple of us had T-shirts on we wouldn't all look the same and as we were a team, and all in this together, he expected us to have a uniformity when we went on to the pitch. I am sure there was also a part of him that thought we were soft if we needed an extra layer in the cold and he wanted to toughen us up. We played in an era when nobody thought to wear gloves, bar the goalkeeper in his gardening/rubber gloves combo, but I am absolutely certain Mr Crotty wouldn't have been able to enforce his dress code on today's kids. I watch games now with several pairs of gloves on view, the odd snood, plenty of undergarments and even some tights or tracksuit bottoms under shorts. When Ben, at the age of seven, ran on to a pitch in Middlesex on a freezing cold Sunday morning wearing gloves, my wife thought it eminently sensible. I squirmed with embarrassment and offered up a silent, heartfelt apology to Mr Crotty.

If someone was trying to get away with a T-shirt underneath their kit, he would quietly ask them to remove it and adhere to the team rules. He never lost his temper or raised his voice, apart from once, in a school gymnasium, and his ire was firmly directed at me.

We would train once a week on a local field; a park would be too extravagant a description. Once the clocks went back and the nights closed in we switched to the gymnasium of a local grammar school. There are not a lot of training drills or exercises you can perform in such a small space, so in the ninety minutes that we had the venue for we would do some sprints and then play 5-a-side. The ideal number to have for the session was fifteen, so that there could be a game going on between two teams of five with the remaining five having a rest. That said, it wasn't too restful, because the only place you could watch that wouldn't get in the way of the game taking place was hanging off the wall bars that covered the length of one side of the room. If you climbed right to the top of the bars you could crouch on the top bar, so at least you weren't hanging like a monkey for the duration of a match.

If we didn't have enough players then Mr Crotty would join in with the 5-a-side and more than hold his own. And this was the scenario we found ourselves in during one such session, when we were at Under-14 level. There were three teams of five in the gym, with Mr Crotty on one of them, and we were playing 'first goal wins'. So as soon as a goal was scored the team who had conceded ran off and climbed the wall bars as the five who had been hanging on for dear life jumped down to replace them and take on the side who had scored. The gym wasn't equipped with actual 5-a-side goals, so we were using wooden benches placed on their sides. It made scoring a goal quite tricky as although the benches were long there was very little height to them, so you had to keep the ball on the ground. We were also playing the rule that the ball wasn't allowed above head height, a rule that always causes huge debate and argument in 5-a-side because each player has a different definition of head height because each player has, of course, a different height. However, the rule does encourage you to keep the ball on the floor, so it's good for getting players to play proper football, but it wasn't good for my natural 'hoofing' game.

Not being allowed to kick the ball high and far was probably frustrating me, at least that is the only rather poor excuse I can come up with for what I did in that session. Mr Crotty was on the opposing team as we started the 5-a-side. On most occasions he would wear a full tracksuit but that night he had ditched the tracksuit bottoms and was going with shorts and socks rolled down to his ankles. It was a look most of us echoed because shin pads weren't required for 5-a-side. Fifteen minutes or so into the session and my team hadn't won a game. We had been up and down those wall bars all night with the odd two or three minutes of football in between. We weren't best pleased. Back down we clambered, ready for another game against Mr Crotty's team, who had been dominant so far.

We were under way again and we were struggling again. We could barely get the ball off the opposition and before we knew it we were in trouble. Again. Three or four quick passes and the ball found its way into the path of Mr Crotty. He was standing on the halfway line. I was the nearest opposition player to him but he was through. All he had to do was run on to the pass and from five yards out knock the ball against the bench and he would have sent us back up the wall bars. He turned and set off towards the ball and as he took his first couple of strides I came in from the side and stuck my foot out. My trainer connected with both his ankle and his unprotected shin. With the ball still in front of him – it was nowhere near either of us when I made contact – he started to stumble. A combination of the pace he was going at and the force of my trip meant he was heading straight for the bench and the wall. If he was unable to keep his balance and he fell, then that bald head was going straight into the polished wood where the ball would probably have gone if I hadn't clattered him.

For me everything slowed down, for him everything probably speeded up. Remarkably he stayed on his feet. I hadn't knocked him out with my reckless actions. I had, though, caused him embarrassment and I had acted like a cocky, stroppy thirteen-year-old prick. Some teammates laughed as our middle-aged coach stumbled and thrashed around for a few seconds and, I'll be honest, I don't think that they really helped my cause. Unsurprisingly he was furious. Puce through anger and a whole lot of effort in trying to stay upright. I was off. Sent off by my coach in a 5-a-side game. I wasn't just off for the rest of that game, I was off for the rest of the session. I was furious too. Embarrassment at what I had done hadn't kicked in by this stage, I was just angry and stomped, yes stomped, off towards the wall bars just to show how angry I was. All eyes were on me as I climbed the wall bars, which was embarrassing because I was never very good at getting up and down the bloody things. I climbed right to the very top and sat there, simmering, for the next hour. I knew I had to apologise. I also knew I had to calm down. Sixty minutes sat high up on a wall bar with your teammates smirking at you is not very conducive to a feeling of Zen, let me tell you.

The session finished. All the other boys left and I was eventually allowed down from my crow's nest. With just the two of us remaining in the gymnasium, the air was calmer and I did apologise and Mr Crotty accepted. Normally these things end with the line 'and the incident was never mentioned again'. Of course in the world of sport things are different and any cock-up, mistake or unsavoury incident is often mentioned again and again and my teammates ensured that the '5-a-side trip' was brought up every week for the next couple of years.

Mr Crotty never mentioned it again; he had quickly moved on. I am not sure I have properly moved on now, nearly thirty years later. I still feel a sense of shame that I tripped him up in a display of such petulance and disrespect. If there are any positives that came out of it, I have always tried to respect coaches since and have tried to instil in my children a respect for the people who are guiding them through their chosen sports. I have also tried to make sure that they keep their own acts of petulance to a minimum.

Ben decided he wanted a 5-a-side party for his eighth birthday. It was a 5-a-side party with about thirty kids, because we were still at that stage where every single boy he knew in the whole area had to be invited, so that nobody felt left out – and also, I suspect from Sara's perspective, so that no gossipy mum could moan in the playground that we had left their son out. Being tight and also being an alpha male, we shunned the football centre's offer of a couple of coaches to help with the party because I said I could do it myself. I wasn't going to coach them of course, they would merely be split into teams and have lots of matches. I was just going to oversee it all and referee if it needed to be refereed. I'd borrowed a few bibs from the club so that we could separate them into teams no matter what football strip they turned up in and as the pitch was quite big and they were still quite small we could easily have teams of eight, rather than five, without it feeling too overcrowded.

The boys were enjoying themselves. When two teams were playing the others could use another area to have a bit of a kick-about themselves, so nobody was left standing around except the parents. Parties for eight-year-olds still fall into that group of parties where you take your children but stay yourself, on account of you either not trusting the organisers to look after your child or not trusting your own kid to behave, or both. It meant that along with an awful lot of children we also had an awful lot of parents, who lined up down the side of the enclosed pitch behind waist-high wooden boards and green netting, which ensured the ball could never leave the field of play.

There is also an expectation at these parties that the child whose birthday it is, is the centre of attention. By the end of the party they must have scored the winning goal, or taken a spurious penalty to win the mini tournament or have been awarded the player of the day award; an added bonus to make their special day extra special. This was the plan for Ben as well. I am not a heartless father after all. We'd get to that final game and he would be the 'hero'. Unfortunately, in an earlier game, it all went slightly wrong.

In an incident reminiscent of myself and Mr Crotty nearly twenty-five years earlier, Ben deliberately tripped up another lad as he was racing clean through. As a referee I was left with no choice, although several people disagree with this train of thought including my wife, but to send him off. Yes, I know it was only a fun game of 5-a-side, and yes I know it was at a birthday party, and yes, probably most relevantly, it was HIS birthday party, but it was a snide, dangerous thing to do.

As he trudged off to the side, maybe in tears, well, definitely in tears, but I am trying to sugar-coat the story in the hope you don't think of me as a bad dad, there were a number of heads behind the wooden boards being shaken in my direction. There were also a few tuts. Even when I trotted out the standard parent line, 'Well he has to learn', the mood didn't improve. In my defence, I didn't send him off and then give him a three-match ban as punishment, he was allowed to return to his own party for all the remaining games. I am not heartless. He also ended up taking the winning penalty and being awarded the player of the tournament accolade. He received a trophy and plaudits and plenty of presents as he should have done. I received the cold shoulder from various family members for the rest of that night and, as they will tell you, I should have done.

As I sat on my own that evening, in a different room to the rest of my family, I needed a cold beer. Keeping control of those children had been hard work. I have so much admiration for all those amateur coaches in all those different sports who do it on a weekly basis. At the moment I must be watching two of my three children being coached in a variety of sports virtually every day of the week. The current sporting roster is planned with military precision and includes football, cricket, gymnastics, swimming, water polo, netball, diving and hockey. Between them they are doing more sports than there are days in the week and we as parents are doing more miles than Lewis Hamilton at a Grand Prix. Most weeks I sit in a traffic jam, cursing one or all of them for us being on yet another journey, going nowhere fast, so that they can train. And then silently I reprimand myself. I tell myself to calm down and remember how much enjoyment they are getting out of it (the sport, not sitting in a traffic jam with their grumpy old man). I also have to remind myself that whatever effort I am going to, it is nothing compared to the effort of the coaches.

What I find remarkable is that across the sports they do their coaches cover so many different ages and backgrounds. In an era when we are often told that the youth of today are 'lazy' and are the 'PlayStation generation', my experience in a variety of sports couldn't be further from that cliché. From the lads who took Ben when he first started at Harrow St Mary's to the teenage daughter who helped her dad with the team to the girls who help Jessie at gymnastics, my children have always had good young coaches who possess both patience and a willingness to pass on their skills and advice.

With gymnastics at the moment, I don't think there is one girl who is coaching Jessie who is over twenty. They are still practising gymnasts themselves and can remember what it is like for these young children starting out. The paperwork and the organisation is carried out by an older lady, the matriarch character of the club if you like, but the coaching is left to the younger ones. It is the same with swimming. Teenage swimmers who are already swimming for the club are giving up their time to drill the younger ones, to pass on what it means to be a swimmer, the hours you have to dedicate to the sport and what the club expects from them. Ditto diving, water polo and hockey. I find so much of what they do impressive. They all have busy lives. They will be studying or working and they will be training themselves, because so many of them are still competing, and I would imagine they would also be quite keen to enjoy some kind of social life as well; and yet they are still finding time to give something back to their sport and to the next generation. They also, in the main, deal with the children amazingly. I'm in my early forties and have three of them, so I should be well practised and experienced, and yet at times I still find looking after them baffling and exasperating; but these coaches regularly display a level of kindness and patience that one would not necessarily expect to find in a teenager.

When the sessions are finished, particularly after gymnastics and swimming, the children are sent back to the matriarchal figure for any loose ends to be tied up and the final goodbye. Meanwhile the coaches are able to gather up their own stuff and put away any equipment, in the case of the gym, or remove the lane dividers in the case of swimming. You may think that

that is quite a banal detail to include in the book, but I see it as a crucial part of the process, because by sending the kids back to the older coach, and by allowing the younger coaches to leave or sort out the facilities, you are removing the opportunity for parents to question the coaches, if you want to put it politely, or lay siege to them, if you don't. You end up picking up your children from the organiser and therefore have to direct any questions to them rather than stomping off across a load of mats or around the poolside to try to find another coach. It allows the coaches to coach and implement what is best for the child without having to worry about an irate or impatient parent trying to tell them that they know better. It also prevents the parents intimidating a young coach just trying to do their best.

Interestingly, with football and cricket there are fewer young people coaching and more middle-aged men. This is by no means a negative although it does increase the parental free-for-all at the end of a coaching session or at the end of a game. There is, however, no difference between the age groups or the sports in the level of enthusiasm shown by all the coaches and the amount of their own time they give up to train our children. Again, these people have full-time jobs, they have families of their own, they have their own interests they want to pursue; and yet despite putting in a full day's work, here they are in a net or on a pitch, fully kitted out and ready to put themselves through hours of dealing with other people's children. Some have more qualifications than others, more coaching badges than others. Some have played to a decent standard, some have been coaching for half a century and will have seen everything in that time. Nothing will shock them, whether it comes from a child or an adult. What links every single coach I have witnessed working with my children is that their hearts are in the right place, they have the best intentions.

This is not always the case of course, so maybe we have been lucky. I was recently told of one football coach who watched as a member of his Under-8s team struggled during a match. Nothing was going right for this poor lad, so at half-time, rather than being supportive and encouraging, the coach stood next to him, shouted at him and told him 'you were so bad you have to wear the pink bib in the second half so everyone can laugh at you.' The lad played the second half in the pink bib. It is a scenario that is played out in lots of professional clubs. The worst player at training has to wear a yellow T-shirt for the next session or something similar. But there are huge differences between this happening with a group of pros and to a seven- or eight-year-old boy.

Firstly, a football club's training session is relatively private. This boy's humiliation was incredibly public, not only in front of his teammates but also in front of the opposition and the parents, who had heard why he was wearing this bib because the coach had shouted at him so loudly. Secondly, I find it hard to believe, though I have no proof, that the colour of the bib was a pure fluke. 'Ooh look, wear the pink bib because pink is seen as an effeminate colour in our macho world of football so some people will think you are a bit like a girl', is, I am assuming, the reasoning behind its colour. And thirdly, and this is the biggest reason why I find this story so appalling, HE IS JUST A BLOODY KID. A small child trying to enjoy a game of football and not doing very well in this particular game. Humiliated, despite trying his best. I am a long way from being able to write a manual on parenting, but in my experience a little bit of encouragement and the odd cuddle tends to lead to better results than making someone a public laughing stock.

Maybe the coach was a dad just doing his best and thinking the stick would work better than the carrot. Maybe the coach thought he was going to be the next José Mourinho and if it was all right for Mourinho to have a rant and a rave on the touchline at a player then it would be all right for him too. Both types are prevalent in the cricket and football coaching world and often the former are forgotten when the latter are criticised in the media. Kids' sport is full of dads, and mums, wanting to give something back to their own children, knowing that, probably, if they didn't stand up and be counted there would be no team for their child and their friends to play for. They don't have the coaching badges that we are told they need because they take time and money to complete and most people don't tend to have a lot of either. They watch their sport, they love their sport and they want to create an environment that will enable the next generation to follow in their footsteps. So they stick on a tracksuit, put on their boots, call the first training session for the squad, stand in front of them and think, *'Shit, what do I do now?'*

At least that's what I did.

Chapter 10

It was a Saturday night and it was dark outside, with the curtains at the front of our house drawn closed and the blind in the back room pulled down to shut out the wind and the rain. Both children were upstairs, asleep in bed. Snuggled on the sofa in front of the curtains lay my wife, television on, glass of red wine in hand, able to relax at last halfway through another hectic weekend. I was at the desk at the back of the house near the blind, glass of red wine in hand, staring at an envelope. The date of this Saturday night is irrelevant because the scene isn't specific. This was how our Saturday nights went for over a year. One of us relaxed, drinking, being entertained by Ant and Dec, Paddy McGuinness or Brucey. The other one stressed, drinking, staring at an envelope. The envelope isn't specific either. The shape, size or colour didn't matter as long as I had enough space to scribble on the back of it. And scribble and doodle and cross out and underline and draw arrows I did. Forget the fabled Anfield boot room, this was the West Harrow back room and it was where I selected my teams for Under-7s and Under-8s football and it was bloody tricky.

From that first game where the parents had discovered the joys of flat-pack goals and ribboned barricades, the boys' team had developed well. They were a good little bunch, none of them difficult to deal with, and the better ones in the group had time for the weaker ones. They didn't get on each other's backs if they made a mistake. They had enjoyed their games, had won some and had lost some, but nobody had given them an absolute tonking. Morale was good. Even the parents were behaving more often than not! The only problem involved our club's father and daughter coaching combination, which was becoming a little bit unreliable.

There is a lot going on for a girl in her teenage years and I found it completely understandable that there were some Saturday and Sunday mornings when getting up early to coach a whole load of kids in the mud and the rain didn't seem a particularly attractive option. Even less attractive if she had been out the night before. There had also been an increasing number of arguments with her dad, nothing unusual in a father–daughter relationship as I am realising – and we haven't reached teenage years with my two girls yet. Some of the arguments were away from the club, some happened during training or matches which didn't help the atmosphere. If only one or other of them turned up then they would need some help from the parents to run things properly.

I was still playing, in the loosest sense of the word, at the time for my Saturday side, and as most games in London take at least two hours to get to even if they are just a few miles away, I would watch Ben's training in tracksuit and boots and go straight to my game from there. Others would turn up clutching the *Guardian*'s weekend section and dressed ready for brunch at the local deli cafe, so it was obvious who was going to be asked first to help out with the boys. I was also keen to help out. I was not a reluctant volunteer. I would be given my instructions by either the father or the daughter, depending on who was there, more often the father, and then we would go off in our little group. It would often be some simple passing or a bit of shooting or working on how to control a football. Nothing too tricky or complicated. We would always end the training with a game or little games and I would referee. No, I didn't send anybody off before you ask.

We were into the final three months of their first ever season and then we had the day that, rather than either one of the father or daughter not turn up on a Saturday morning, neither of them turned up. And that is how I ended up, tracksuit on, boots on in front of a group of kids thinking *'Shit, what do I do now?'* There were also parents watching. I could say they were looking on expectantly but I would say the looks on their faces suggested they were thinking *'Shit, what does he do now?'* A few were also thinking *'let me get to that cafe, order a macchiato and open the* Guardian *as quickly as possible before he ropes me in.'* So with a group of boys, a group of parents and a two-hour training session all before me, I decided to keep things simple. A quick jog and a stretch, for the boys not the parents, and then one big game, again for the boys and not the parents.

I thought that was keeping it simple and trouble free. It didn't turn out like that. A two-hour training session doesn't look like a lot when written down, but when you are in the middle of it and meant to be running it and when you have very little clue about what you are really meant to be doing, it goes very, very slowly. The jog and the stretch amounted to around fifteen minutes of the session, so that left us an hour and forty-five minutes for the game. Absolutely ridiculous! For the professionals, a game only lasts ninety minutes, and at the level the boys were playing at their games last just an hour, split into three twenty-minute periods.

To expect them to play a game of football for that amount of time was naive at best and stupid and lazy on my behalf at worst. I learnt very quickly that morning that even in one training session, the boys at that age needed to do a variety of things. Keep it as just one thing for too long and they get bored. And boy did they get bored!

We were fine for the first half hour or so and then it started to fall apart. A parent who had been walking their dog round the park for the first part of the session came over to watch, immediately distracting a couple of the boys who wanted to go over to pat and play with the animal. Seeing a couple of teammates showing a lack of interest, a couple more who hadn't been seeing much of the ball during the game decided to chase each other to try to knock each other into the mud. This then provoked frustration from the rest of the team as they conceded a goal due to the fact that two players were stroking a dog and two were trying to knock seven bells out of each other. As it was so easy for the other team, a few of them stopped trying. A couple just stood talking to each other and one of the quieter members, left isolated, was kicking at the ground with one of his boots and chewing a nail through his glove. A lot of them wore gloves. I needed to get a grip and restore order and more importantly interest. I needed one big sharp blast of my whistle to get them all in to me, have a chat and then go again. Except of course I didn't have a whistle, on account of the fact that I wasn't expecting to be taking a coaching session for seven-year-old children.

I bellowed. Even the dog jumped. The boys came in to the middle of the pitch and gathered round me. I have no idea if they were expecting words of wisdom or a bollocking. They got neither. Instead I did what a lot of coaches seem to do when they need to buy themselves some time to think, I told them to go and get a drink. Off they ran to their pile of water and Lucozade bottles, trying to trip each other up on the way.

I called over a couple of the sportier-looking dads.

'We've got to do something different with them. They are bored already. If we split them into smaller groups could you take a group each?'

They agreed but none of us knew what we were really doing. We tried to remember a couple of the drills that we had seen over the Saturday mornings when we had been standing watching, in between mouthfuls of bacon sandwiches. Our recollections were vague as we had all been on our phones and paying little attention, so we decided to resort to what always worked in our respective gardens. Shooting practice with a dad in goal. The boys would stand in a line and take turns to run with the ball, then pass it to one dad who would then pass it back to them. They'd take one more touch and then shoot at the goal guarded by the other dad. In simple terms, we were playing 'Beat the Goalie'. If it had been a school fete, there would have been a coconut up for grabs if you scored; well, if it was the 1950s.

It wasn't a highbrow drill, it probably wasn't in a coaching manual, but it was fun, it was something different, the boys enjoyed it and it stopped them clumping each other. The rest of the session passed off relatively peacefully and free of distracted boys who wanted to do something else. We drew it to a close and gathered the boys and the parents in. All looked to me to say something. Our coaching duo usually said a few things about the boys: who had trained well, how well they were all doing and other snippets of positivity. They would also reconfirm the details for the game the following day. Expectant faces looked on. What words of wisdom could I come up with?

'See you tomorrow. Meet nine thirty here. Kick-off ten o'clock. Bye.'

No words of wisdom as it turned out. I was knackered. A hot bath, a pub lunch and an afternoon on the sofa would have been perfect. Perfect but impossible as I had to go and play for my Saturday club team. Not surprisingly my performance that afternoon was slow and lethargic. This had nothing to do with me taking the training for the boys. Every time I was turning out now I was slow and lethargic. At twenty-five I had been slow and lethargic, so it was hardly surprising I was slow and lethargic at thirty-five.

It was a lost weekend for our father and daughter coaching duo as they didn't turn up for the game on the Sunday morning either. I stepped into the breach once more and with more gusto and enthusiasm than the day before at training, because I knew if I was responsible for the boys I wouldn't have to put the goals up or disentangle myself from the ribbon barrier. I had the much simpler task of kicking the ball around with the boys until the opposition turned up and were ready to go.

For this game I didn't change anything from the previous regime. Isn't it ridiculous that even though I'm a dad managing a bunch of boys in a kids' game of football that I still slip into managerial clichés? I had watched our coaching duo at several games, I knew where all the boys liked to play and that, with rolling subs, the idea was to give all the boys a similar amount of playing time. The game passed off like any other: plenty of goals, a couple of kids in tears, plenty of mistakes, somebody who wasn't the goalkeeper picking the ball up in the area because he didn't know the rules and all outfield players in the same square yard of the pitch trying to get the ball. None of it surprised me because I had been seeing it at every game I had watched Ben play in for the past few months. What did surprise me was how loud and clear the comments made by the parents of both teams were. Rather than being alongside them, when you are the coach you stand on the opposite touchline. I could hear everything and of course if I could hear everything then the children could hear everything. The parents were behaving well; they weren't directing criticism or anger at the boys, they were just contradicting themselves constantly.

'Get rid of it!'
  'Hold it!'
  'Shoot!'
  'Pass!'
  'Get wide!'
  'Stay where you are!'
  'Push up!'
  'Drop deep!'

None of it said with malice, all of it said to try to help the boys, but of course none of it did. At that age, the boys are constantly looking to their parents on the touchline for approval. Any kick, any pass, any shot, any tackle, any run would be accompanied by a look to the sidelines to see the reaction of mum and dad, closely followed by a look to the other sideline to see the reaction of the coach. At the same time parents wouldn't want to be seen to be just focusing on their own child, so would offer encouragement to the other boys, but that might contradict what their own parent was saying or even what the coach was saying. And if you think that this paragraph is confusing to read then try being six or seven with all of that swirling around your head and in your ears while you are trying to play a game that you are very much still learning.

We muddled through the next few weeks – sometimes both coaches would turn up, sometimes one or the other, sometimes neither. It became obvious to all parties that we couldn't continue in this vein because it wasn't fair to the boys. I had stepped in when they hadn't turned up so, by default I guess, I took over the team with the season drawing to an end. Rather than say I, I should definitely say we. As anybody involved in amateur sport will tell you, coaching and managing are just a small part of running a team or a club. There is a tremendous amount of administration to do. Having been the fixtures secretary for my club for a couple of seasons I was not keen to revisit that world.

We had four teams at the club I played for and every week I would have to confirm our fixtures with our opponents. Each team would be playing a different club so there would never be block fixtures for all four teams against one club. Each week I would be confirming kick-off times, venues and potential kit clashes. Each week I would get a scalding from a fellow fixture secretary, who had been doing the job for twenty-five years at least and wasn't impressed that I was phoning on the wrong day or at the wrong time.

Didn't I know that the league had set rules for fixture confirmations and didn't I know that I wasn't following them?

Yes, I did know that but I did have a rather busy life with a job and kids and I wasn't sitting around in my slippers and cardigan all day waiting for calls from fellow fixture secretaries.

The hassle would continue until Saturday, when members of my own club would call to find out where they were going because they hadn't read the email properly or had written the postcode down wrongly, and the opposition contact for teams coming to our ground would ring me because they were lost or the handbook they were using was an old one and we had moved grounds. At the same time I was trying to get ready for my own game. The whole thing was, to use a technical term, a ball ache. I didn't want to go through all of that again so I did what I always do when there is something needing to be done but I don't want to do it. I asked my wife if she would handle that side of things. So that is why I should say WE took over and not I took over.

The season didn't have long left to run and with nobody else deemed suitable it was decided that we would not only look after the team for the rest of the boys' time as Under-7s but also through the summer of tournaments that had been lined up for them: and then on to their Under-8s season. All of a sudden this wasn't just helping out on an ad hoc basis. It wasn't just a kickaround in the park with them, or a kickaround in the garden with just my son, this was putting me in charge of their footballing welfare. If I had always felt responsible for passing on my enjoyment of sport to my son then those feelings were now being multiplied fifteen-fold. I now had a whole squad of boys looking to me every weekend. Their weekends were all about football. I had to make sure that their weekends stayed all about football. I viewed it that if any of them stopped enjoying it then that would be my fault. I wanted it to be fun and exciting and exhilarating. The boys didn't care about that, they just wanted to beat every side that they came up against.

The footballing authorities can decree that all games are friendlies until the children reach a certain age. They can decree that there are no league tables, no titles, no promotions and no relegations. They can insist on respect banners and pre-match handshakes between all team members but what they can't stop is children being naturally competitive. They want to win. As far as my squad were concerned not only did they want to win, they were also going online to look at the league's website. All the scores were published there, as well as in the local paper. A lot of them were stat obsessed and so would compile a league table themselves, based on all the other results. They knew where they were in their league table. They knew who the best teams were. They even knew who the top goal scorers were, because they were keeping a tally of those as well. This was very much a competitive situation for them.

I actually think that the attempt to keep league tables and the like out of the children's game at an early age is aimed squarely at coaches and parents. It encourages the coaches to try to develop their players rather than striving to win every game so that they can say THEY have won a title or promotion. The authorities are hoping that by removing the competition element, coaches won't just tell their players to give it to the best player or the biggest player or the quickest player and let him do the rest. That instead the coach will take a more holistic approach. They are also hoping that parents might stay calmer if their children aren't in a battle for a title or close to being relegated. That is quite a forlorn hope and before the Under-8s season started I knew I had to begin with the parents and not the boys.

We had just about got through to the end of the Under-7s season and had more or less survived the summer tournaments, but before we began our new season I thought it was important that we were all thinking the same way. Thank goodness the parents were receptive, because if they hadn't been my time as coach would not have lasted too long. I wasn't going to tell them off or shout at them, mind you, I just wanted to suggest that they changed their behaviour.

'You are such an enthusiastic group of parents and your willingness to make every effort to help your sons with their football is admirable and that's what makes our little team so special,' I said, thinking that it would be best to start with compliments, albeit true compliments. They returned my look thinking *'we know he is starting with compliments, albeit true compliments, just so he can criticise in a moment.'*

'The problem is . . .' I began.

'Here we go . . .' they started thinking.

'. . . that we are confusing the boys a bit,' I continued.

Ironically the parents then looked confused.

'I know we are all meaning well in what we are shouting, most of the time, but it is a little bit contradictory.'

If you are thinking it is odd that I can remember exactly what I said then I should tell you that I am not relying on memory here but on the piece of paper I still have from that day. I was so nervous about saying this and getting it right that I wrote everything down.

I went on to tell them that all we needed was encouragement. Nothing else. 'Well played, great tackle, great shot, great pass, unlucky boys, fantastic goal, don't worry about being eight nil down lads we can still get back into this.' Those kind of things. What the boys didn't need were instructions, and conflicting instructions at that, coming out of different mouths. Without wanting to be self-important, although it will come across as this, I made it clear that instructions would have to come only from me. Even if they were wrong – which, I assured the parents, they would be; saying it several times because I was winging this as I went along (the coaching, not this beautifully prepared speech) – at the least the boys would be getting one clear message. Instructions from one side of the pitch, encouragement from the other.

There were nods all round. So far so good. Now on to the second bit, which I thought for some might be harder to grasp.

'Winning isn't going to matter.'

A few looks of confusion but not many, so I moved quickly to reassure them.

'Don't worry we aren't all going vegan, wearing homemade football boots and singing "Kumbaya" before kick-off, but the approach might be slightly different. Our aim as a whole group is to improve the boys as footballers. Nothing more. We want to make them better at tackling and running and heading but most importantly we want to make them better with the football. We want them to improve their dribbling and their passing and their tricks. They will lose the ball, they will make mistakes, they will concede goals but they will be getting better with the ball and in later years you will hopefully see how comfortable they are when they get the ball. I want to make sure that every boy here will be a better footballer than me. I can hoof it, I can head it and I can kick people in a tackle, but I can't dribble and I can't perform a single skill.'

I thought by ending it in a self-deprecating way that it might show we were all in it together. I didn't consider that some of them might then think *'Well if you can't dribble and can't perform a single skill, what the bloody hell are you doing coaching my son?'* If they were thinking that then I am truly grateful none of them said it.

'So we are about encouraging and more specifically encouraging them to play and to work with the ball. What we don't want is them getting it and then hoofing it.'

I focused on one particular parent. Our group was full of different people from different backgrounds. The boys were a glorious mix of older siblings, younger siblings and only children. Some were state-educated, some private, some at religious schools. We had parents who had been together years, we had single parents, we had parents going through separations. We had black, white and Asian. We had parents who played football, we had parents who played other sports, we had parents who didn't have a sporting bone in their bodies but had produced children who did.

The dad I was looking at wasn't at the sporty end of the spectrum. He often arrived on his bike to training and the games, while his wife brought their only child in the car. He was one of the older members of the group and his son was one of the less athletic ones. Both were enthusiastic, dedicated and never missed a training session or a game. The only problem was that any time his son received the ball, and often when other players received the ball in a defensive area, this dad would bellow 'Get rid! Get rid!' It had the desired effect on his son who would then launch it into no man's land.

'Could we please,' I asked him, but with the whole group still around, 'never ever say get rid of it again? If you are fighting the urge to issue that instruction then "pass it" will do. We don't want any of the boys to be afraid of the ball, no matter where they receive it on the pitch. If they try and play out from the back and lose it and the opposition score then so be it. In the long run that will be better for them than just getting rid of it.'

He was a lovely man and had no problem with that message and neither did the rest of the group. Everybody understood what we were wanting to do. There are a lot of times in youth sport when coaching the parents is as important as coaching the boys and now I am the parent all of the time and never the coach, I do wish for more communication from my children's coaches. Tell ME what I need to do to help you coach my kids.

While I knew what I wanted from the parents and I knew what I wanted from the boys, I still wasn't really sure how to train them. That summer between Under-7s and Under-8s, I searched high and low for, or to put it another way Googled, training sessions for children. I also went to meet the FA at Wembley Stadium. You could take this as a sign of my dedication: however, that would be stretching it somewhat. I had been hauled before them, not for the first time as you will discover later; this time it was for a discussion I had had on the radio at the World Cup in South Africa.

England had been thrashed 4–1 by Germany in their last sixteen game. The tournament had been a miserable footballing experience as Fabio Capello's side struggled out of a group containing Slovenia, the United States and Algeria, finishing second behind the Americans and thus giving them that tricky match against the Germans. The subject of how our players are coached from a very early age all the way through to the professional game had cropped up again and again on the shows I presented. After the defeat in Bloemfontein though, all hell was let loose through the medium of Chris Waddle's mouth. He ranted about the state of youth football, he ranted about the coaching, he ranted about facilities. He ranted and ranted and ranted and he struck a nerve with people listening. He struck a nerve with me as well, as this was the summer between the Under-7s and the Under-8s and I backed him on a lot of the things he had said. The FA thought we had misrepresented them and after several conciliatory emails flying back and forth I found myself in a room at Wembley Stadium, with a mug of instant coffee in front of me and one of the heads of grassroots football.

By the time I left, I had been given numerous figures to show how much the FA were investing in grassroots football, that coaching badges weren't nearly as expensive as I thought, though that isn't to say that they don't still cost a lot of money, and that there would be more funding in the future. I had also been given a coaching manual that the FA had developed to use with children. Lots of drills and lots of sessions and lots of ideas. I had some material to work with.

Chapter 11

I pored over the book during the summer, handwriting several different training sessions on to scraps of paper. I didn't want to turn up at training holding this huge manual I had been given; I would have resembled Michael Aspel about to surprise some Z-lister on *This Is Your Life*. It would also have looked like I was trying too hard or, more to the point, like I knew what I was doing. Manual or not, I was still wet behind the ears in this role.

We hadn't trained during the off season. There had been some tournaments for the boys to keep them going, but after throwing in holidays and the fact that we believed as a club that the boys should not be doing football all year round and that they needed to experience other sports, it became clear that regular training sessions were unnecessary and would have been poorly attended. We waited until the beginning of September before we were up and running again.

I arrived early at the park for my first ever official training session. There was no need for the tracksuit, just T-shirt and shorts and socks. I'd gone for the white shorts and white socks; old pre-season training habits die hard. I'd also moisturised my knees heavily so that they weren't as white as my kit, not that anybody would be drawing a picture of me. I had bought a whistle over the summer, so I wore that round my neck on a piece of string. In my head I was the image of a dynamic young football coach, about to set my team off on a season of (uncompetitive) glory – in reality I looked more like Mr Baxter, the old PE teacher who was a mainstay of *Grange Hill* in the 1980s. My shambolic look was completed by bits of paper tucked into the waistband of my shorts. It was good being dressed for the summer and it was fine writing my training session out rather than carry the big book around: the problem was the two did not go together, as I had no pockets for my notes.

I had copied three different drills out of the book for this first training session and with regular glances at my notes I began setting up the requisite poles and cones for each one. I had chosen one drill for tackling, one for passing and one for shooting. With nobody else around yet, I set everything up myself with relish, not the reluctance I felt when first told we had to put up the nets. I was genuinely excited. I knew what I wanted to do, I had put real effort into working out what we were going to do and I wanted this to be the start of something special.

Boys and parents arrived, all the regulars from the previous season and a few new ones as well. The boys took themselves off for one big kickabout, the parents went for a coffee. In my memory I always thought I took my time getting a coffee and a sandwich, when I was just a parent. That I didn't rush back outside to see what the coaches were doing, that I would rather relax and have a chat than intimidate them by watching every single thing they were doing. I probably didn't. I probably did exactly what the parents did that morning – rush in, grab drink and food and be back outside in the blink of an eye to see what exactly was going to happen to their little treasures in the hands of the coach. The boys were still just having their kickabout.

I called the boys in. They sat down in front of me. Their parents stood behind them. We welcomed the new boys. That was the easy part. Pairs of eyes bored into me from every direction, expectancy in the air for the first training session of a new season. As ridiculous as this may seem considering we are talking Under-8s football here and not the Champions League final, it was intimidating. I explained to the boys, and by default the parents, what we were going to do that morning. There were nods and murmurs and thankfully nobody shouted out 'what are you doing that for you amateur clown?' I grabbed a couple of the dads who had made it known they were willing to help out, told the rest of the parents to stay where they were and took the boys off towards the collection of cones and poles.

After rummaging around in my shorts for a few seconds I pulled out the scraps of paper for the drills and explained them to the dads. I then told the boys which drills they would be doing and having split them up into little groups I sent them off to the respective areas. If I thought things hadn't run smoothly at that very first training session, when I just got them to play a big game, it was nothing compared to what followed.

Hindsight is a wonderful thing, but three different activities with a couple of dads helping out and a group of boys who hadn't trained for a while and some of them training with the club for the first time was maybe slightly ambitious. Actually, it was very ambitious. I had also picked a couple of exercises that were aimed at an older group of children, so my boys didn't have the ability or the understanding to do what I was asking. There were balls flying everywhere, cones being moved, bibs going on, bibs coming off, children shrugging rather than running, questions being asked rather than instructions being given to teammates. It was chaotic, although given I had spent so much time planning everything, I could at least call it organised chaos. I sent them off at regular intervals for a drink, to try to regain some kind of control of the morning, while studiously avoiding eye contact with any parents, particularly the new ones who must have been wondering what they had signed their children up for. We ended that morning with some games of 5-a-side and guess what? They worked like a dream. Who would have thought that simple small-sided games of football rather than over-complicated drills would have appealed to seven- and eight-year-old boys?

Again, I know this is not the professional game, I know it's not even *Football Manager* on the computer where you pretend you are a professional manager, I know it is just kids' football but I spent the rest of that day mulling over what had happened. Where had I gone wrong with the training? What was wrong with the sessions? I revisited the coaching manual to look at alternative drills to see if there were others that would work. How should the boys train the following week? Should they work on the same things or should we look at different skills? However I answered my own questions, I realised during the course of that afternoon that it all came down to one thing. I had simply been too ambitious and too egotistical. The coaching session had been a way of demonstrating that I knew what I was talking about. I hadn't run it for the boys and aimed it at their level. What I needed to do was keep things simple, keep things fun and build up slowly. I didn't learn my lesson.

Our first game of the season arrived. Expectant parents on one side of the pitch, me and the boys on the other. Nothing but positivity expected and required. The boys were excited and the parents equally so. We had a squad of ten. Seven could be on the pitch at any one time and you could make substitutions whenever you wanted, as often as you wanted. The game was split into three periods of twenty minutes with a break between each one. The boys had warmed up properly and by that I mean they hadn't lost interest once. A bit of passing to each other, a bit of running and stretching because they had seen the professionals do that and they wanted to copy it and then a bit of shooting with one of the dads passing the ball to each one of them before they took a touch and then hit it. It was important to have a dad involved in that bit because if he wasn't then the boys would have all been taking shots from two yards away from the goal, scoring every time and leaving us with a dispirited little goalkeeper before we had even started.

And before we started we had to jump through some official hoops. There is a lack of trust in youth sport, which is always centred around age and size. I guarantee that you can go to any sporting event, at any age group and there will be somebody there, be it coach or parent, grumbling in hushed tones about an opponent.

'Look at the size of him/her,' whispers random dad to random mum.

'I know,' whispers random mum back to random dad, while checking all around to make sure that the parent of said object of their conversation wasn't within earshot.

'They can't be in the right age group,' dad continues. 'They're cheating. That boy/girl is too old.'

'Sshhh,' replies random mum, worrying that random dad could well get chinned by the parent of this child or at the very least get into a heated argument.

'Some children are just bigger,' she says trying to placate him. 'They develop at different rates. Just because he/she is bigger than our little darling doesn't mean they aren't the same age. Everybody hits puberty at different times.'

'They are seven years old,' counters random dad, wondering whether to confront someone over this to make sure his child isn't done out of victory.

'And anyway,' continues random mum, determined to stop her husband causing a scene, 'we have a couple of big kids in our team.'

'That's different. We know they are the right age and we would never cheat.'

It's always the opposition and never us. No matter what the sport and no matter where we live.

To try to prevent these conversations, although unsuccessfully in my experience, identity cards were introduced for each boy. So not only do they, or rather their parents, now have to remember their kit, their boots and their water bottle for each game, they have to remember their ID card as well. Before the match, both sides are lined up and then the coach of each team goes over to the opposition. He receives a bundle of ID cards from their coach and then shouts out the name of each player. That player then steps forward to acknowledge his name and as a coach you check the picture on the card with that of the lad who has stepped forward. When the big one steps forward, you try not to register your surprise that despite being nearly six feet tall his identity card indicates he was only born eight years ago.

The opposition coach is doing the same with your team and when the whole process is complete you get your own batch of cards back and hand them back to your own parents, while at the same time convincing them that the big lad playing for the opposition really is the same age as their own child.

'He can't be.'

'He is.'

'But he is massive.'

'I know he is but the birth date on his card is right for this age group so we have to assume it is all legitimate.'

'They're cheating.'

'No they're not.'

'Well there's something not right.'

'I've got to go. We're about to kick off.'

The identity card procedure doesn't rid the parental touchline of the 'age of the opposition' debate. It merely adds the notion of fraud into the discussion.

With the parents still discussing the legitimacy of some of the opposition's players the game began. We decided we were going to play with two defenders, three midfielders and one striker, plus of course our goalkeeper. We kicked off.

A cacophony of shouts from the opposing touchline. 'C'mon Harrow!' cut through the autumnal air.

'Pass it!' yelled the dad who had been told he couldn't say 'get rid of it' any more. 'Pass it!'

The boys eased themselves into a game that was as helter-skelter as you would expect from a load of seven-year-olds. I was aware that one of the big things in kids' football is to make sure that at such an early age the children didn't see themselves as being able to play solely in one position. Yes, the majority of them wanted to be the goalscorer, but it was important that they tried different positions. For years I had read about the famed Ajax youth system. The Dutch side would ensure that as the players progressed through their academy they would play in all positions on the pitch at some point. The benefits were several, including the obvious, that a player who thought he was a central midfielder, for example, might suddenly discover an aptitude for being a right-back. Until a player plays in a certain position, how do you know if they can or can't play there? Also by playing in an unfamiliar position, a player will gain an understanding of what the regular person who plays there goes through. What he sees, what he requires, where he needs his teammates to be when he receives the ball and so on and so forth. If it works for Ajax I thought, then it can work for Harrow St Mary's.

Ajax, however, had perfected this system over several decades, using some of the best professionals and experts in the world game and tapping into the insight and know-how of some of the greatest international players to have played the game, not just in the Netherlands, but globally. They weren't, to the best of my knowledge, relying on a middle-aged dad with only amateur footballing experience.

I made my first substitutions, bringing my own son off first. I didn't want to be THAT coach who was accused by others of favouring his own child. Of course by not wanting to be THAT coach, I became THAT OTHER coach who is unbelievably harsh on his own child, much more so than on the others in his charge. And if you are reading this Ben, that is an apology of sorts.

So with my son and two others off, and the three substitutes on, the game continued.

'Pass it!' came the constant cry from the parents opposite. They had also started to relax, so much so that they had begun to gently rib the referee. A referee who, fortunately, was one of their own. At this level of football, the home team provides the referee for the game, sometimes a parent, sometimes a coach, always a lightning rod for accusations of bias.

We had chosen Mark to be our referee for the season for a whole variety of reasons. He was enthusiastic, he loved his football, he always had a smile on his face, he was great with the kids and he was massive. Unless you were brave or stupid, or both, you wouldn't want to pick a fight with him. The one other reason, however, was because his son was part of the squad. The previous year, when Mark hadn't refereed, he would get so worked up watching his lad play. Like all of us, he had this over-whelming desire to see him do well, and he couldn't hide it. He never shouted or got angry with his boy but you could feel the pressure around him and in turn you could see it affecting his son. Slowly but surely he was going into his shell, shrinking, not wanting the ball in case he made a mistake or missed a chance at goal. He wasn't alone in this, but he spent a lot of the match looking over towards his dad for either instructions or approval rather than concentrating on the game. By making his dad the referee, we managed to stop all of that. His son couldn't always make eye contact with his dad or seek his approval because his dad was busy elsewhere on the pitch and at the same time Mark couldn't concentrate only on his son. He had a game to referee and that demanded his full attention. If he had then turned out to be hopeless we would have had a problem but he turned out to be sensational. Relaxed, grinning and empathetic. He always had a word for both sets of parents, the opposition coach and most importantly the players. He encouraged and cajoled both teams while refereeing. He didn't rule by the letter of the law, he used common sense. If a disorientated child picked up the ball, and it happens more often than you would think, he would deal with it sensibly, not immediately pointing for a penalty or giving a free kick. If a child made a mess of a throw-in or a corner, i.e. didn't take it properly, then he would allow them a second chance rather than awarding the ball to the opposing side. If there was a late tackle, he wouldn't be getting out his cards, he would be making sure there was an apology and a handshake and everybody moved on. Soft or sensible? Wishy-washy and lenient when he should have followed the rule book? You can decide for yourself but all I know is that the way he officiated gave us a lovely atmosphere in which to play football.

'Pass it, pass it!' continued the dad on the other side of the pitch. I made more substitutions. Confusion started to affect the boys. They were struggling to remember where they were meant to be playing on account of being told to play several positions. When I had brought one off, for example, he had been playing as a striker, but when I sent him back on I was asking him to play in defence, and yet this had slipped his mind and he was still ambling around in the opposition's penalty area rather than his own. He wasn't alone. It was a pattern that repeated itself over the first few weeks. We would start well, play some really nice stuff and then collapse once I started making changes. They say that a manager can really earn his money with his substitutions. Mine weren't earning me money, simply causing widespread panic. It took me a month or so to realise it, but once I did that is how I ended up at the back of my house, every Saturday night, with a glass of red wine and the back of an envelope.

The substitutions needed military precision planning. I needed to be organised and I needed to be fair. My aim was that by the end of the season all the boys had played roughly the same amount of minutes and in a variety of positions. I also wanted to make sure that each boy had worn the captain's armband a couple of times (yes, we had an armband for the captain, boys do like to copy the pros). Finally, we also had more boys in the squad than were allowed on a match day so every week a couple of them were 'rested'. We tried to tie this in with the boy going away or being needed at a family occasion. As a very disorganised man this was a huge test for me and involved me creating a spreadsheet for the first time since my business studies degree. Of course it never ran smoothly, because a parent would always get the date wrong for when they needed their lad resting and throw the whole thing up in the air.

I planned way in advance who was being rested and who would be captain, but as regards the positions and the substitutions, that was done with the accompaniment of wine on the Saturday night. If I started with a boy in defence and then substituted him, how could I make sure when he came back on that he remained in defence? If we had two or three players stronger than the others, how could I rotate it to make sure that they weren't all off the pitch at the same time? One boy in each game would have to be substituted twice, so how could I make sure it wasn't the same boy I had substituted twice the week before? I tried to answer all such questions on the back of my envelope with doodles and squiggles and plenty of crossing outs. It wasn't an exact science but I hoped over the course of a season it was fair and didn't cause the disruption we had seen in our early games.

Even with all that pre-planning there was still plenty to test my ambition of being fair to everybody and to try my patience. Parents would get lost on the way to an away fixture so a boy would be late, immediately rendering my enveloped plans redundant. Even worse if two or three of them were in the same car. There would also be illness or injury on occasion, leaving the envelope torn up and blowing across a field like confetti being thrown over a bride at a wedding.

Then, of course, you have to deal with distraction. If a player, for whatever reason, has little interest in the game, do you keep them on even though it could cost their teammates? And at this age they can be distracted by the smallest of things.

My friend's seven-year-old boy would go week in, week out to his football training and then play at the weekends, usually as a goalkeeper. He didn't have a great interest in the sport and he didn't have a great deal of aptitude for it either. He was persuaded to stick it out by his dad because he was making new friends and it got him out of the house and doing exercise. My friend would go and watch his son every week, but one weekend he was going away for work so he asked his dad if he would like to go and watch his son.

'Of course I'd like to watch my grandson,' he said.

'Great,' my friend replied, 'although I do need to warn you before you go to watch.'

'Warn me, about what?'

'It's nothing serious.' My friend realised he had alarmed his dad. 'It's just that you shouldn't set your expectations too high.'

'Well I'm not. I do realise it's just a game of kids' football.'

'Yes, just don't expect too much from your own flesh and blood. He has a problem concentrating during the game. Don't be surprised if he's chewing his fingers or wandering around in his own area rather than watching the game. And don't get exasperated if he does. That's just how he is sometimes. Football might not be his thing but at least he is trying.'

'Understood,' said his dad.

Game day and grandfather and grandson set off for the football, laden with kit, food and drink. The boy runs off to join his teammates and the grandfather takes his place behind the respect ribbon on the touchline. The game begins and just as the grandfather had been told the small boy starts to nibble on his gloves and run around his area. When the ball is in the vicinity and the boy is called upon to do something, he makes a couple of decent saves to the delight of his grandfather, who is now starting to wonder why his own son had been quite so harsh on the boy. With the ball at the opposite end of the field to the boy, the grandfather took out his phone to text his son to report on the positive performance so far. When he looked up the ball was starting to travel back down the pitch. His grandson could be about to be called into action again. Except, his grandson was no longer in the goal. He looked at his phone and then looked back up again, believing his eyes to have played some trick on him first time around and that his grandson hadn't really disappeared.

But he had. The ball was heading towards the goal and his grandson, the goalkeeper, the last line of defence, was nowhere to be seen. Out of his right ear, he heard a rustling. He looked down and there was his grandson trying to get into the bag, still wearing his goalkeeping gloves.

'What are you doing?' he asked in a slightly raised voice. 'You should be in goal. They are about to score.'

'I am getting a biscuit,' replied the boy, in a tone of voice that suggested he couldn't quite understand why he was being asked such a ridiculous question.

'Why? They are about to score.'

'Because I am hungry,' he said in the same tone of voice, believing the question to be no less ridiculous than the first.

There wasn't much else for the grandfather to say as the ball slammed into the net and the hungry boy's teammates looked around wondering where their goalkeeper had gone. From a manager's point of view, you can do all the planning, write on all the envelopes, try all the training sessions, be as fair as you possibly can, rotate the subs and the positions and encourage parental positivity but you can never account for a child with a pang of hunger.

I started to master the art of substitutions as the season progressed. They didn't affect the games as much as they had done at the start of the campaign. My spreadsheet confirmed that the boys were all being treated fairly as regards minutes played and number of times as captain. Except one. I couldn't shake the habit of being harder on Ben than the others. If I needed to do something to balance things up then Ben would more often than not be the one to suffer. It didn't happen very often but just occasionally if I had gone wrong with a substitution or made a mistake with the player I was resting, then Ben was the easiest option to solve it. I preferred him to be moaning at me rather than another parent. It was hugely unfair on him and wrong of me and I should probably still be apologising to him even now.

We won some, we lost some, we drew some. Results and score lines don't stick in my mind because they really weren't important. It mattered to the boys of course and to give them a boost we would send the score, the goalscorers and the man of the match to the local paper in the hope that they could see their names in print and get a boost from it. The paper would often print them, but they would often also get the team name wrong or the boys' names wrong and on the odd spectacular occasion both the team name and the boys' names wrong, thereby making it a completely different match report which did not really provide the boost we were hoping for. We would send the scores in when we had lost as well, so that our goalscorers would still receive recognition, even in defeat. We didn't have to write match reports for detail wasn't needed and I was very grateful for that after one particular game.

The name of the opposition is irrelevant. In the twenty or so months that the boys had been playing games we had never come up against this team. The boys had had some tough games in that twenty months and already, after such a short time, matches against a couple of other clubs had already seen an intense rivalry develop. This either came through the two sides being evenly matched or through the historic rivalry between two clubs. It is both odd and endearing that boys will come and go from clubs and yet a game that was full of needle and very tetchy between Club X and Club Y some thirty years ago can still be full of needle and very tetchy nowadays, because that rivalry has been passed down from generation to generation at both clubs. I was not from the area, none of the clubs we played had any significance to me and yet I would find myself geeing my boys up more than usual before the game against the 'big rivals'. And when we beat them 3–1 and 5–2 I found myself jumping higher and celebrating more when we scored. And yes, that whole paragraph was included just to pat myself on the back and record in print my two wins over the local rivals.

Anyhow, I digressed to blow my own trumpet. This new opposition arrived at our ground and began warming up. Our boys were doing the same. We went through the rigmarole of checking identity cards, of everybody shaking hands and then went our separate ways. As ever we had plenty of parental support, the opposition likewise. The opposition had also chosen to do what several teams had been doing, which was to have a coach on either side of the pitch. This was perfectly allowable, and so their main coach actually stood on the same side as the parents, with his assistant on the same side as me. The game kicked off.

'Pass it!' came the immediate call from parents, even though we didn't actually have the ball.

'Keep it!' shouted their coach from in among his own parents.

They couldn't do that for very long and the ball went out for a throw-in. We took it. One of my defenders controlled it and slipped it to one of his teammates in midfield.

'Smash him!' came the shout from within the throng of opposition parents.

I ignored it. I could have misheard. It could have come from anybody. We kept the ball.

'Pass it!' I knew who that had come from.

'C'mon get stuck in. Hit him, hit him hard!' I stared over towards the touchline. The coach was separate from the rest of his parents and the instructions were definitely coming from him. His assistant, on my side of the pitch, remained resolutely silent. The pattern continued throughout the half; aggressive comments when we had the ball, less of them when they had the ball. Referee Mark caught my eye on several occasions but we didn't feel there was a great deal we could do about it. Besides, the shouts were affecting my set of parents rather than my team. The boys were trying to concentrate on their football and also the opposition fortunately weren't carrying out the instructions of their coach. There was the odd foul, but nothing malicious and nobody had been 'smashed', to use his vernacular. My parents were more distressed because they were concerned that one of our lot could get injured if they were 'hit hard' and also because this aggressive coach was in their midst. They were caught between saying nothing and hoping he'd shut up, or saying something and risking it escalating on their touchline.

We reached half-time with the score all square and in that very English way we did not complain to the coach about his behaviour. The boys were still calm, unlike their parents, so I talked to the parents more than to the team. They were angry and on the verge of saying something and while I could understand their sentiment I still wanted to stay silent. The boys were comfortable and hadn't been lumped up in the air. Yet.

When he began the second half in the same vein and with the same words, some of the parents could take it no more. Concerned that if they didn't say something, that if they didn't ask him to refrain from telling his players to 'smash' ours, there would be a serious injury, a couple of the dads asked him to stop. It will not come as a surprise to you that their requests were not entertained by the man and he became irate because of my parents' intervention. In the course of the discussions on the touchline, I could hear from the other side of the pitch the obligatory phrase in this situation.

'Well, it's a man's game.'

Not at eight years old it isn't and while I wanted my team to tackle and head and get stuck in and if necessary commit the odd foul, I didn't want them to injure an opponent deliberately. He probably didn't want an injury to one of my players either but his 'encouragement' was more likely to lead to one. As the 'discussions' continued between parents and coach, the boys became more and more distracted. A couple were getting quite distressed so I had to bring them off. Another game in which the envelope system was knackered! With concentration gone, substitutions awry, parents arguing and the chance of somebody getting hurt hanging in the air, it was no surprise that we were thrashed in that second half. I couldn't wait for it to finish.

Mark blew the final whistle, with discussions still audible on the far touchline. There was too much noise and commotion going on to be able to calm the boys so I called them in and then walked with them a good fifty yards away from the pitch and away from all the adults. We all sat down; it wasn't a team talk that required me standing up and looming over them. We spoke about how they had done well, how they had tried to ignore everything and kept playing football and that even though it hadn't been nice there will always be people in games who want to kick you rather than play football against you and that it was important to learn from this. As my words of wisdom continued to flow, I felt a tap on my shoulder. I looked up and there was the opposition coach. He stretched out his arm and offered his hand,

'We're off, so I just wanted to come over and say well played.'

I hesitated while I thought things over in my mind for a good couple of seconds, keeping my hands firmly where they were, then I picked at the grass between my legs and said 'Nah, you're all right', and turned back to my boys.

'You are a fucking disgrace,' he said. This was spoken in a strong Cockney accent, so strictly speaking it was more 'You are a facking disgrace'. 'What kind of example is it to set to the kids if you won't shake my facking hand?'

Thinking it was probably a better example to set than facking swearing in front of a load of kids, I thought I would get up and try and usher him away. This immediately disappointed the boys, who were giggling having heard the F-word twice in a matter of seconds, and despite the threat of violence that had hung over their game and was quite possibly hanging over their coach right now, they were starting to think that this was one of their funniest and best Sundays of the entire season. As I tried to move him out of earshot, not easy with a few of the boys trying to follow so they could still hear, he continued.

'I'm going to report you.'

'Report me? To whom?'

'The League. I'm going to report you to the League.'

'For what?'

'A lack of sportsmanship. For not shaking my hand.'

'Fair enough, but I didn't think your behaviour during the game was sporting so if you are going to ask your team to smash mine, I don't want to shake your hand.'

'Oh, fack off.'

I didn't want to lower myself to his level, or rather I did want to lower myself to his level but I didn't want the boys to know I had done so, so I muttered in hushed tones, 'No, you fuck off. Now.'

And he did. Feeling brave and tough and pleased that I had seen off this man through a combination of taking the higher ground and my own potty mouth, I turned back to the boys. Only then did I realise that several of the parents had seen what was going on and had made their way over, as had referee Mark. As he was twice the size of anybody else at the park that morning, it was probably his presence, rather than mine, that made the man leave.

The match was brought up in conversation regularly as the season headed to its conclusion. By the parents still recovering from their first brush with thuggery at a kids' game and by the boys, still delighting in hearing some proper hard-hitting swear words. As far as I know, I wasn't reported to the League, or if I was then they didn't take any action over it. Not that they could have done much about it because I would be leaving in just a few weeks. I was moving out of the area and heading back North and so my time as a football coach would be coming to an end. The demands of work had already led me to miss the odd training session and when I was back in Manchester I knew that I would definitely not have the time to look after a side. We had a few more games to go, followed by the club awards ceremony, and then I would be out of there.

There is no romantic ending, there was no unbeaten run until the end of the season with goals flying in from all angles. There was no Cup Final victory with me being carried aloft on the players' shoulders at the end for masterminding the win, because as you know there were no competitive games, plus I was fifteen stone and a whole group of eight-year-olds wouldn't have been able to lift me. But even if there was no romantic ending, there were at least a couple of moments that, and I hope you don't think I am going overboard here, brought tears to my eyes.

I had enjoyed every single second of my year with the boys and felt very fortunate to have watched them improve individually and grow together as a team. I hope they felt that they had been fairly treated, though maybe Ben didn't, and some who had started off the season believing they could only play in one position were now flourishing in other areas of the pitch. We weren't world-beaters, we didn't win every game, but we gave it a damn good go and bar that one game we always tended to head off for a Sunday lunch, wet and cold but happy. If at the start of the season we had some strong players and some weak ones then by the end of it the weaker ones had very much closed the gap. We had moved on from worrying about which combinations of player were on the pitch at the same time.

Even though our final game was played in the springtime, the weather remained steadfastly English. Wet, grey and cold. The parents had turned out in force, because it was their last opportunity to bid me farewell. Again, the opposition is irrelevant. The score line is irrelevant. In fact everything is completely unmemorable about that morning bar one thing. Remember the son of the dad who shouted 'get rid, get rid' before we encouraged him to change it to 'pass it, pass it'? Well, he had progressed beautifully during the course of the season and had turned into a tough-tackling defender who was difficult to beat. He had slowly but surely stopped 'getting rid' of it whenever the ball arrived at his feet and was always trying to pass it to a teammate, even in difficult situations, which we encouraged him to do.

In that final game, the ball was played over the top by the opposition. My reliable defender saw it go over his head and chased back towards his own goal in pursuit of it. The striker for the other team did the same. By the time they reached the ball it was in our own penalty area. Nine months ago we would have heard 'get rid' and he would have lumped the ball out for a corner or a throw-in. Now I thought I knew what he would do. He would look up and try to pass the ball back to our goalkeeper, and if it went wrong then so be it. But he didn't do that. He went to pass the ball back to the goalkeeper with his right foot but at the last moment he stopped and dragged the ball back past his left foot and in doing so turned himself through one hundred and eighty degrees. The bemused striker was left in his wake as our defender brought the ball away and then passed to one of his teammates. He had performed what is known around the world as a 'Cruyff turn'.

I jumped high into the air. I cheered loudly. I pumped the air and I applauded. When I looked across the pitch there was his dad, with his hand over his mouth, eyes wide, being patted on the back by the other parents. Some reflected glory for him, in among the surprise. The boy looked at his dad and then looked over at me and smiled. Not a smile that said 'Don't worry, I knew what I was doing' but a smile that said 'Wow, I've just made a lot of people very happy.' He had made me the happiest of the lot. Nothing else mattered in the game after that, that was the pinnacle of the season. With the match drifting towards its conclusion, I consulted my envelope for a final time, signalled to the referee to make my final ever substitution and brought off my son.

It all ended with the awards afternoon. A giant marquee full of trophies was set up in the park, with plenty of stalls and activities set up too, to raise money for the club and to keep the boys interested. All the teams in the club were there but you didn't have to sit through everybody else's awards, only your own. As the coach, I was able to pick the number of prizes we would have. I could go one of two ways and create so many awards that every boy was able to win one – from 'Top Goalscorer' to 'Player who left his boots behind on the least number of occasions' – or I could just go with the traditional few and not try to reward every single boy through the creation of patronising categories. I chose the latter: it would also save money on the engraving. So we had 'Top Goalscorer', 'Most Assists', 'Most Improved Player', 'Manager's Player of the Year', 'Parents' Player of the Year' and 'Players' Player of the Year'. The first four I either chose or worked out, the last two I obviously didn't, and I made sure the votes were collected and counted by somebody else, just to make sure everything was above board.

I gave a very short goodbye speech to the parents and the boys, aware that the attention span of the younger members of my audience was not great and also aware of a prickly feeling in the corners of my eyes as I began. I really didn't want to cry in front of them. I quickly moved on to the awards, with Ben winning the 'Most Assists' award. No matter how many times I added up the figures on my spreadsheet, I couldn't alter that fact. I had to give him the award. I'd worry about the favouritism accusations later. The other awards were announced and handed out and we were left with the 'Players' Player of the Year' trophy. I was handed the envelope, unaware of its contents.

'The Under-8s Players' Player of the Year for 2010/11 is . . .' I opened up the envelope and smiled. 'Ben.'

A season of worrying that I was favouring him, a year of him probably (definitely depending on who you talk to) being treated more harshly than the other players by his grumpy coach, a year of highs and lows and arguments over why he was wearing gloves when I never did, ended with an award for him, given to him by his mates. Lads that he will hopefully remember for many years.

THE LOVE OF THE GAME

A season that ended with me feeling so grateful for the experience, so grateful to the boys and the parents for all the support they gave me and a season that ended with my boy holding a trophy and me with my arm around him posing for a photo. We weren't a coach and a player in that photo. We were father and son. No, we were a very proud father and son. And that was how it was going to be from now on. I was back to being a parent. No longer a coach, simply a parent.

Chapter 12

Mr Poole's voice reverberated around the building. Other classes, other parents could easily make out the instructions that were aimed at us; and not just instructions, there were rebukes, plenty of rebukes. He was appropriately named for a swimming teacher but his voice, rather than the temperature of the pool, would send shivers down our spines. His wife, Mrs Poole, had been my first teacher; a kind, genial, patient woman, soft of voice and of manner, who had looked after us in the baby pool. Only when we could swim the width of that pool, ten metres, and had the badge to prove it were we allowed to move into the bigger pool down the corridor. The bigger pool was out of sight from the baby pool, so until you were actually moved up a class the only thing you knew about this promised water was that there was a man with a very loud voice in it. The legend of his authority and strictness had been passed down from generation to generation, so that once children were aware that they were moving up 'into the big pool' they would beg their parents not to put them in his class.

I was no different. I pleaded with my mum to find any other teacher at the leisure centre to take me through my twenty-five metres and fifty metres badges but my pleas fell on deaf ears, which is ironic really; Mr Poole had a booming voice and shouted at his classes because he was hard of hearing and not because he was tyrannical. Only after leaving his charge were children ever made aware of this fact and of course they were not going to pass on this prized information. If they had had to spend the last few months being shouted at and scared stiff then they were going to make sure that those who followed in their strokes and kicks were going to experience exactly the same thing. Of course all the parents knew, but they never told their children either, because they believed that as long as the kids thought he was strict and scary they would behave themselves in his lessons and learn to swim more quickly. It was a win-win situation for all bar those in his class. Sadly, he retired shortly after I had been moved up out of his class and so I was never able to pass the legend on to the children who followed me.

The bigger pool, or the training pool to give it its correct name, was always split into three sections, with the shallow end reserved for the children who had just moved up out of the baby pool, the middle section for the intermediates and the deep end for those children who had to wear their pyjamas and spend most lessons diving for a brick. By the time a child had picked up that brick and turned their pyjamas into a float, their work in the training pool was done. It took me a while to get to that final stage, not because I was a weak swimmer, but because I found it difficult to tie knots in both legs of my pyjama bottoms and then blow into the waistband to inflate them. I either struggled manfully with the knots so that by the time I came to try to inflate the pyjamas I was gasping for air and out of breath, or I thought I had managed the knots quite easily and started blowing, only for the damn things not to inflate because the knots had come apart. It required strength, stamina and patience, none of which I have now let alone in the early 1980s. By the time I eventually completed that final exercise, or they felt sorry for me and just passed me anyway, I am never quite sure which, I had the full set of badges. To go with the ten and twenty-five metres, I also had the fifty, hundred, two hundred, four hundred, eight hundred and fifteen hundred metres ones. The final one is the only one I can remember because at the age of ten or eleven it felt like it took me about half a day to complete. The brick and the pyjamas routines were all for the 'safety awards'. There were three of those in total – bronze, silver and gold – and once they and all your distances were completed you didn't need lessons any more and you could walk out of that training pool for ever. And that's what I did at the age of twelve. And now, over twenty-five years later, I was back.

I walked up the same ramp and past the same bicycle stands that had been there all those years ago. The imposing desk and barrier were still there to greet me as I walked through the entrance. The vending machines were still in their same positions, over in the far right-hand corner by the stairs that took you up to the viewing gallery for the public pool and the 5-a-side court. Vending machines still crammed with everything you shouldn't eat, just rebranded and renamed since 1985. There were even the iced drinks machines, albeit in a different place. Just walking through the doors made me yearn for a packet of beef flavour Monster Munch and a Slush Puppie. But whereas I had walked out of those doors two decades ago with a bag over my shoulder, I was walking back in holding the hands of my two children. They had been learning to swim down South, but now we had moved back to Manchester life had come full circle and I was going to be watching them exactly where my parents had watched me.

Jessie would be starting in the baby pool where Mrs Poole had looked after me and Ben would be in the training pool. As we walked into the changing room, I was waiting to hear that booming voice echoing around the place. Of course it didn't. Mr Poole was long gone and people of his age teaching the children were long gone too. Whether in the baby pool or the training pool, the poolside was full of bright young things, all identically dressed in navy blue T-shirts with INSTRUCTOR in big white letters on their backs and dark blue shorts and flip-flops. All of them closer to the age of their pupils than the parents watching. Gone were the older members of society who taught my generation in a ragbag collection of seventies sporting gear – which wasn't retro back then, but just a few years old.

The two of them progressed through the levels quickly and I noticed how advantageous it was for my daughter to have a sporty older brother. Whatever he achieved in a sport that they were doing together she was determined to achieve it too and achieve it at an earlier age than he had. If he was in the class with the purple swimming caps by the age of nine, she wanted to be in it by the age of six. If he completed his fifteen hundred metres badge when he was ten, she was telling us she was going to do it by the age of seven. It goes back to the age-old argument that no matter how hard some adults try to remove the element of competition from children's sport, you can't remove the competitive nature of children. Ben had four classes to progress through before he had completed the course and Jessie had every class to progress through, as she was starting in the bottom one at the age of four. When a child completed a level, they were moved into a new class and given a different coloured swimming cap.

That was one of the few things that had changed at the place. Everybody had to wear a swimming cap. I don't think I've ever worn a swimming cap in my life and as my children would have attested when I struggled weekly to pull them over their scalps, it showed.

We would drive home after a lesson and Jessie would be in the back of the car. Strapped into her booster seat, she would say, 'I've got to get to yellow at the end of this term, Daddy.'

'That's great darling.'

'I'm fed up of being orange. I want to be yellow.'

'Mmmmm,' I replied, as I listened to the radio, had thoughts about what I was working on next, looked out of the window or wondered why the driver in front hadn't indicated.

'So do you think I will be yellow, Dad? Dad? Daaaaaaaaaaady?'

'Sorry. What?'

'Do you think I will be yellow?'

'Do I think you will be yellow? Eh?' In my mind I'm wondering if she's talking about the Simpsons, 'What? What do you mean do I think you will be yellow? Yellow in what?'

'In swimming.' She had learnt at a surprisingly early age to roll her eyes at me and her timing was good as well, because she would wait until mine met hers in the rear-view mirror.

'Yes, you could make yellow.' Colours and caps were dominating our swimming landscape. Surprisingly, for once in kids' sport it wasn't a commercial scam either. The caps were provided free, so parents were not expected to dip into their pockets every time their child moved up. By the time they hit the middle to upper classes on the course there was a light blue, a dark blue, a violet and a purple cap. Subtle differences and not easily told apart. Certainly not easily told apart when you are trying to pack a swimming bag in that tight amount of time between school finishing and a swimming lesson starting; and rather than getting rid of old swimming hats we had kept the lot.

'Daaaaaaad, you've brought the wrong hat.'

'No I haven't. It's purple and you're in purple now so I haven't.'

She replied with a hint of exasperation and what felt like a lot of condescension. 'Yes, you have. I am in purple but that's violet.'

'Violet is purple. It's fine.'

'No it isn't. Violet was the class I was in last term and now I'm in purple.'

'Well we haven't got purple. Violet will do, nobody will notice,' I replied in hushed tones, not wanting any other fathers and daughters to be privy to my telling off from a child not far off out of nappies, while at the same time trying to stuff her clothes into an unfeasibly small rucksack that we had to use because it had 'Hello Kitty' on it, or some other such nonsense, and cursing the organisers who thought it sensible to use two very similar colours for two classes at different levels.

'They *will* notice.'

'Well tough,' I said, yanking it down over her curls and wishing it could go a bit further and cover her mouth as well. She stropped off and the kids did notice, of course they did, but she coped and then mentioned it every day for the rest of that week. The following week my dad took her, with the right coloured hat, but it took him nearly fifteen minutes to get it on to her head so she missed half her lesson. She never complained about me again after that.

Ben was progressing serenely through his classes, helped by the fact that he would put any old thing on his head as long as he could get into the pool and swim. He had been a water baby, in a pool from just three months old on a family holiday. He equated family holidays with being in the water. Even when swimming wasn't on the agenda, he had fallen into that pond. Other members of the family were less inclined to get into the water after an unfortunate incident at Center Parcs when he was just two years old.

As well as loving being in the pool, Ben had discovered water-slides at Center Parcs. The problem for him was that being so small he couldn't go down them on his own, so he needed to go down with me. Now taking a child down a waterslide is quite a technical task. You need to go fast enough so that you don't get stuck and cause a traffic jam behind you but you can't go at full pelt because you have this small person with you. You also have to make sure you have a firm grip on your child because you don't want to leave them halfway up the slide as you carry on and you have to lift them fairly high so that they don't take a lot of water in the face and panic. Finally, as you approach the end of the slide and get ready to plunge into the water, you have to hold them nearly above your head so that the impact of you hitting the water doesn't knock them loose. I tended to lie on my back all the way down, holding Ben aloft and just to my side, and then as we approached the last turn, sit up slightly so that our entry into the pool was gentle.

We stood at the top of the slide, Ben in an all-in-one Lycra swim-suit, short-sleeved and down to his knees, his swim nappy bulging beneath. I managed to convince the lifeguard that I would be OK taking him down with me – my son, not the lifeguard – and off we went.

'Again, again!' shouted this little voice as we crashed into the pool.

Back to the top we went and back down the slide we went, sev-eral times. Different members of the family stood at the bottom to watch us come into the pool and praised Ben's bravery for coming down the slide. As we finished one run and climbed out, my sister said she was going to come with us. We climbed the stairs, queued to get to the front and then I offered my sister the chance to go ahead of us or after us. She chose the latter.

We pushed off and then I lay down and held Ben up and just to the side. We started to gather pace and went around a couple of corners with him laughing and giggling as he had on all our previous descents. And then that bulging swim nappy started to move. Maybe it was too full, maybe with all the tumbling about in the water it had become less elasticated. The reason was unimportant, the result was that a small piece of poo was now working its way out of the swimsuit and into the tide of water. I moved my son just that little bit further to the side. Out it popped, straight out of the nappy and the swimsuit and landed on the slide in the water.

There was nothing I could do. I couldn't stop the poo and I couldn't stop us on the slide as we were moving too quickly. Equally I had no great desire to scoop up my son's poo and bring it down with us and finally I knew that it wasn't going to be some poor unsuspecting member of the public who was going to slide through my son's tiny pile of excrement, it was going to be my sister. So that was fine.

For us as a family, both when I was a child and now as a parent, swimming has been about having fun. Inflatables in the pool, throwing balls, diving headers off the side and going down slides, though not having a poo on them. The lessons were there to make sure you could swim properly and be safe in the water. Having come to the end of his lessons and completed all of his badges, including the one involving the brick and the pyjamas, because they still do that one, Ben came out with the statement that every parent dreads.

'I'd like to do swim training.'

I don't have a very good poker face, but I needed it here. I needed my face and even my tone of voice to be encouraging, while masking my inner panic.

'My teachers have been impressed,' he continued, 'and think I have a chance.'

'*Have a chance to completely ruin our family life,*' I said silently in my head while at the same time saying audibly out of my mouth, 'Well, that's great Ben, we can investigate that.'

He was so excited on the way home, he was so excited as he burst through the front door to tell his mum, whose own poker face was appalling. She couldn't mask her horror. She had a good friend whose daughter starts her swim training at five in the morning. That's not get out of bed at five in the morning, that's dive into the pool at five in the morning. I had interviewed many a swimmer and swim parent for the BBC over the previous few years and I was well aware that swim training takes place either early in the morning or late in the evening. Swimmers would always thank their parents in those interviews because of the sacrifices they made. Lack of sleep, plenty of food preparation, odd meal times, travelling around the country, hours sitting watching your offspring going up and down a pool were all coming our way to replace normal getting up times, time with our other children, glasses of red wine, Netflix on the sofa, takeaways and more glasses of red wine.

We received the training times from the club. The earliest he would have to be in the pool would be six in the morning. Early, but at least it wasn't five. It also wasn't compulsory. There were plenty of sessions throughout the week, either side of the school day, and as long as he could make at least a couple a week, we were told, he would be fine. Of course it wasn't as simple as just turning up at the pool and him diving in and getting on with it.

There's a lot more to it than that. We would leave for a training session looking like we were going to move house. He'd need food for straight after the session and at least two water bottles, one for during the session and one for afterwards. There'd be a bag with his school uniform in, another with his swimming equipment in. Swimming equipment you say? Surely that's just trunks, towel and cap? Oh no, I would say back to you. It is trunks, towel and cap but also goggles, two types of float – one to be held, another to go between the legs – and some flippers. We'd also throw in a spare pair of goggles because every month, without fail, he would manage to break a pair. Also, without fail, I would stand and watch each training session and marvel at how my boy had gone from pooing on a waterslide to managing length after length of butterfly, while wondering at the dedication and ability displayed by him and all the others in that pool.

This was more than just length after length of swimming. They worked on stamina, they worked on strength, they worked on technique. Most of each session was spent in the pool but they also had gym work timetabled in, along with stretching sessions. I was torn between thinking this was too much too soon for my ten-year-old son and admiring how much he was throwing himself into it, how determined he was to complete a press-up or a plank. This was more than one step up from my attempts at football training sessions. This was designed to build them up, to develop their bodies, to make them race ready for the club so they could represent it in a swimming gala.

Off to Wigan we went. Known for its pier and its rugby league, it was the venue for our first ever swimming gala. It was a cold winter's Saturday afternoon as we allowed the satnav to guide us into the town centre and towards the local baths. As we got closer, struggling to find a parking space, I could see several middle-aged men walking towards the venue in shorts. I am well aware of hardy Northerners, but with the heating cranked up in the car the bravado of some people seemed ludicrous.

As with all children's sporting events, the registration process is designed to be as chaotic as possible. It doesn't matter whether it is a football tournament or a cricket festival, a swimming gala or a gymnastics competition, the sole purpose appears to be to create the maximum amount of discomfort and confusion for both parent and child, although mainly for the parent. As with all of these things, there is never just one queue. Sometimes you have to join a queue depending on your child's age, sometimes it will depend on which county or area the club is from, sometimes it will be completely random just because they can. Finding the right queue is one challenge, keeping hold of your own child is another because any more than two minutes in a queue and they are bored and off trying to find their mates. So as you edge closer to the registration you are scanning the whole venue trying to find where they have buggered off to because if you don't have them with you when you reach the desk, you can't register them. With bags, children, coaches and parents in abundance, I managed to keep hold of Ben. With him ticked off a list, he went in one direction to find his coach and club mates and I was pointed in the direction of the spectators' gallery.

I dodged through the assembled throng. I would love to have said slalomed to make it sound really poetic, but I was carrying a bag of dry clothes and snacks for him for afterwards, a spare water bottle of course, and my iPad, because I was concerned I might get bored: so with all of that, and because I was wearing several layers of clothing, I wasn't able to move with my usual alacrity. Finally I reached the stairs that would take me up to the viewing gallery and despite being weighed down I took them two at a time. At the top of the stairs, the arrows on the wall pointed around to the right. As I came round the corner I saw a room full of spectators. Stationed in the room were various stalls: some offered food and drink, others the opportunity to buy swimming gear at a reduced rate. Blocking my way into this room, and the viewing gallery beyond, was a trestle table and behind that two ladies perched on rickety collapsible chairs. On the table was a plastic margarine tub full of loose change, a couple of books of raffle tickets, a huge stack of pamphlets and two travel mugs; one of the essentials of a sporting administrator, due to the large amount of time they are not allowed to leave their stations.

Thinking that I didn't want to enter a raffle, I started to make my way around the table and into the room.

'Excuse me sir,' said one of them, in a voice loud enough to make the people nearest the table turn around.

'Oh, it's OK,' I said, 'I don't want to enter the raffle.' I used the same apologetic tone that we all use when approached by charity canvassers in the street. Polite but firm, coupled with trying to keep walking so that you don't get stuck.

'Oh, it's not a raffle,' she replied equally politely and equally firmly. 'You have to pay to come in here and you get a raffle ticket as part of the entry fee.'

'An entry fee?' Quite a lot of the people were still looking in my direction.

'Yes, it's three pounds sir, and with that you get a raffle ticket and a programme.'

As the people in the room continued to think that I had tried to get in without paying and gave me disapproving looks accordingly, I hurriedly picked three pound coins out of my pocket and handed them over to the lady. I gave her my name, for the purpose of the raffle ticket, not to go on a blacklist of people who tried to blag their way in, and also received one of the pamphlets. Calling it a programme was going overboard for a sheet of A4 folded in half with a lot of typing on it. Adding it to the pile of objects I was carrying, I stuffed the raffle ticket into a pocket, still none the wiser as to what I could win. I headed towards the coffee counter craving some warmth, with the chill of the outside winter air still in my bones and as I joined another queue I dissected the last few minutes. Here I was about to part with some money for a service and a product. The people behind the counter were going to make me a coffee. I was paying for their time and also the coffee, milk and hot water required for the beverage. Two minutes earlier I had paid to watch my own son in a swimming race. He was not a professional, and to the best of my knowledge nobody else in the gala was a professional, and yet I had been charged an entry fee. I bought the coffee for £1.50 and left the counter thinking *I've paid good money for this so it had better be hot and strong*' and as I headed to the viewing gallery I applied the same principle: '*I've paid three quid for this, son, so you had better put some effort in.*'

Arms now full because I had added a coffee to the mix – if I could have found a cabbage I would have won *Crackerjack* – I crashed through some more double doors and into the viewing gallery and the warmth hit me immediately. I was grateful for it at first as I doubled back on myself and climbed up five stairs and surveyed the area. The viewing gallery stretched the length of the pool, had seven rows of seats and was heavily populated. If a seat wasn't occupied by a person, it was occupied by a bag or a coat. If it wasn't occupied by a personal possession then it was being kept by someone as a favour to somebody else who hadn't yet arrived. I loitered at the back, unable to see a free seat that was easily accessible.

And then I felt it. A bead of sweat starting to make its way slowly down my back followed by another and another, all trickling down under my T-shirt, thick winter jumper and heavy winter coat to the waistband of my jeans. I was wearing several layers in what was essentially a public sauna. And while I was boiling, the men I had mocked on the way in for being in shorts and T-shirts on a winter's day in Wigan were nice and comfortable. Not a drop of sweat on them. I was the novice swim parent in a viewing gallery full of experts. Not only were they all dressed for the occasion, vest tops and sandals for the women in case you were wondering, but they had all come equipped as well. There were iPads and smartphones to distract the smaller children who had been dragged along, and cool boxes and food hampers for the adults. People were obviously in it for the long haul and with a sinking feeling I looked down at the pamphlet. There were over seventy races. Over seventy. In a panic, I went straight to the final race and scanned the list for Ben's name. It wasn't there. Thank God, we wouldn't have to stay to the bitter end. The races were categorised by age, by stroke, by distance and by sex. The youngest ones would always go first in each stroke, building up to the eldest. I went through all the races involving Ben's age group. Out of the seventy plus races on the card, he was in two of them. Was I excited for him? Of course. Was I honestly also thinking *this is going to be a long afternoon*? Of course. And was I also thinking *that's £1.50 per race*? Absolutely.

I took off my coat, but not my jumper. I was stubbornly refusing to acknowledge that I had made an error in my choice of outfit, even though nobody else on that balcony cared. Several of them had now got clipboards out of their bags, had attached the race order pamphlet to them and were studiously making notes. Mine was creased and already had the odd coffee stain or sweat mark imprinted on it. I was not going to be making notes and while still feeling boiling hot I also felt a sense of freedom. A freedom that would allow me to enjoy the events that were about to unfold, no matter how long they were going to take. That freedom came from the knowledge that none of this really mattered. Yes, I knew that Ben would want to win his races, but I also knew that he wouldn't be that bothered if he didn't. I knew the sports that really, really mattered to him and that although he loved his swimming it wasn't the be all and end all and that enabled me to relax as well. In fact I relaxed to such an extent that by the time his first race (number thirty-one on the order of events) had finished, I realised I had been cheering on the wrong child. In my defence, there were no lane numbers down at the poolside, so I had no idea whether lane one was at the top of the pool or was the lane nearest to me. To counter that, you could argue that after ten years I ought to be able to spot my own son, but from a distance, with all of them in black trunks and goggles and not all wearing swim caps to identify the club they were swimming for, it was harder than you may think. Having said that, the lad I was cheering on won, so maybe I should have realised that it wasn't Ben! And that isn't as harsh as it sounds because even at such an early age you could see the ones for whom swimming was their main sport. Ben performed admirably and in his other race I cheered him on accurately to a respectable second-placed finish, but for him this was just going to be something he did for fun.

He wanted to stay to the end, to know whether his club had won and to be part of the camaraderie. They didn't win but it didn't matter and as we left he asked for crisps and chocolate and a McDonald's on the way home rather than the healthy snacks his mum had sent me with. I acceded to them all. As we walked back to the car, joking that I had cheered on the wrong child and laughing about the parents who had been taking it seriously with clipboards, he was saying he'd like to do it again.

We got into the car and headed home, listening to the football scores on *Sports Report*. Then we talked about what we were listening to; a surprise win here, a thrashing for another club there. We got his McDonald's and as he stuffed another chicken nugget into his mouth I told him how nice it was to see him smiling after his races, enjoying himself and not having a face like thunder like he so often did after football or cricket. He told me how nice it was not to have his performance analysed in the car on the way home for once. It turned out it was one of the best three pounds I had ever spent.

Chapter 13

I had a maroon rucksack over my back and I was dragging a bag full of cricket equipment with one hand and carrying a set of spring-loaded stumps in my other. Bounding off in front of me, carrying his bat but nothing else, was Ben. We were off to the nets, father and son. He wasn't yet into double figures and we were a couple of years away from him being able to bowl me out. Despite his young age he had decided that cricket was his thing. From being four or five, he had fallen in love with it. He would play it whenever possible. We could just be walking down a street and he would suddenly turn his left arm over and bowl a make-believe delivery at a startled pensioner coming the other way. He would search it out on television instead of watching the programmes aimed at his age group and I didn't discourage it. The abundance of stats and averages and run rates helped his maths no end – with each over lasting six balls he grasped his six times table in no time at all. I confess that I also didn't discourage it because it gave me an excuse to watch sport under the guise of helping his education.

He had started playing early at a great club but unfortunately under a terrible coach. A man who had favourites and who constantly focused on the negatives and what a boy couldn't do rather than praising the things that he could do. When the parents of his favourites suggested at the end of the season that we all club together to get him a gift, I reluctantly contributed a tenner. When they told me that they were expecting a little bit more because they wanted to buy him an iPad, I steadfastly remained at a tenner. An iPad? Give me strength. What was wrong with a bottle of wine and some Quality Street?

The negativity was affecting Ben's confidence. Rather than praise his bowling, which rarely erred in accuracy or pace, and I am trying to be objective and not just a proud dad, he concentrated on his batting which was more hit and miss. Mainly miss. So to try to help him, we were going to the nets. I don't really want to get too technical here, on account of the fact that this book isn't a cricket manual and I am not a cricket coach, but Ben's problem, according to this man in charge of his team, was that he was trying to smack everything and in trying to smack everything he was aiming to hit the ball to the side his legs were on, rather than the side his bat was on. In cricket the side your legs are on when batting is known as the leg side, while the side your bat is on is not the bat side but the off side. His coach wanted him to be more technically correct and hit the ball on the off side . . . so that was what we were going to work on.

We reached the nets, located in the furthest corner from the car park in the same park that he played his football in. They were empty as we lugged, or rather I lugged, the equipment over.

'Do you want to bowl as well this afternoon?'

'Yeah, because I want to get you out loads.'

'Oh you do, do you?' We were still at the stage where I could control whether he got me out or not.

'Yes, Daddy. I can get you out every ball and I can smack any ball that you bowl at me,' he shouted back, as he picked up the pace to reach one of the places where he was happiest in the world.

'We'll see about that,' I said, knowing full well that I could allow him to do that for the whole time we were there. So why didn't I? Knowing that his confidence was low, knowing that his coach wasn't being great with him, knowing that he just loved cricket and wanted to play it, why didn't I let him smack the ball around for a bit, bowl me out a few times, laugh and joke and generally enjoy the sport? Why didn't I? The only answer I can come up with is because I was his dad.

As he prepared himself for batting, I got the net ready. It was scruffy, there were damp leaves scattered through it, even though it was summer, and the AstroTurf surface had seen better days and was worn through, nearly to the concrete beneath in places. I put our stumps at the far end and then walked back down the net, stopping halfway along to drop the maroon rucksack. Removing some red plastic cones from it, I went back down towards the stumps. Then I placed two or three cones on the off side for when he came in to bat. I wanted him to either hit the cones or hit the ball between them. That done, I went back to the rucksack and removed the dozen or so red cricket balls we had collected over the past year. In he waddled, this small boy weighed down by cricket equipment. He had on oversized pads, his batting gloves and a helmet. I wasn't going to be bowling bouncers at him but he wanted to replicate the batting conditions in a game, and the players all had to wear a helmet. So bouncing and bubbly and weighed down only by his equipment and not expectation he arrived at the crease. I explained the point of the cones I had put out and what we were trying to achieve.

Trying to achieve – I am shouting at myself as I write this. 'You twat!' I am shouting. 'You are the dad of an eight-year-old in a cricket net! Have a laugh! Don't try to achieve anything except having fun!'

He nodded and nearly fell over as the movement of his head, combined with the weight of the helmet, caused him to stumble forward.

He regained his balance, took guard and I threw the first ball down to him. Stepping across, he thwacked the ball over to the leg side.

'That's a four, Daddy. First ball, I've hit a four.'

'Yes, Ben, but you didn't hit it where I asked you to hit it, did you?'

'But it was a four, so it doesn't matter.'

'Well it does, doesn't it? We're here to work on you hitting it to the other side so that you don't get out as much in games and you'll be happier and your coach will be happier.'

Why I cared about the feelings of his coach I have no idea, especially as I was already hurting the feelings of my son. Beneath the grill of his helmet, I could see a mixture of confusion and disappointment.

Second ball he missed, third ball he missed, fourth ball he missed and the ball hit his stumps. He had gone from carefree and happy to frustrated and sad in the space of four balls. He wasn't the only one. I should have ditched the cones. I should have allowed him to smack the living daylights out of every single ball and not worry about where it went. His confidence was low when it came to batting so just feeling leather on willow would have helped him in that net session. He could have claimed four after four, six

THE LOVE OF THE GAME

after six and he would have got home and told his mum that he
had hit an unbeaten hundred against Dad in the park. But I didn't.
I persisted. And it got worse. I moved the cones around, tried to
come up with different exercises and drills, but little worked. In
the end I resorted to bribery, which unsurprisingly was the most
successful tactic of the afternoon.

'I'm going to throw you down ten balls, Ben. If you hit seven of
them through the cones on the offside, I'll give you a treat.'

'What treat?'

'How about fifty pence?' I just stopped short of adding 'shiny',
which would have turned me into a character in an Enid Blyton
novel.

'No.'

'No?' How could he not want a whole fifty pence?

'Some Match Attax. That's what I want.'

'Please, that's what I want PLEASE.' Looking back I may have
been too harsh on his batting but I wasn't too harsh on his man-
ners. He had to be polite. He still does. At this point I ought to
explain what Match Attax are. But I can't. Despite them clogging
up our house for several years I still don't understand them, how
they work or the games the kids play with them. They are football cards basically, Panini stickers for the new generation.

'OK, a pack of Match Attax for seven balls through the cones.'

'No,' he countered, shaking his head, which caused less loss of
balance than nodding. 'Five packs of Match Attax for five balls
through the cones.' He couldn't bat for toffee but his negotiating
skills were bang on.

'OK, OK, OK.' I just wanted to get on with it. 'Deal.' Needless
to say, not five, but all bar one of the balls went through the cones
and by pure fluke he went home happy because he was getting
some Match Attax. I should have gone with the bribery straight

off. At least I understand bribery, whereas I have never really understood batting. My role in any cricket team I have played in has been to bowl and leave run scoring to someone else. A lack of ability and a fear of being hurt have always kept me very low in any batting order with both myself and my teammates crossing everything that I wouldn't be needed. So even in the nets, I should have understood my son's joy at whacking a four, because I rarely did something similar.

I went to what is called a cricketing school, a school that has provided many cricketers for Lancashire County Cricket Club and the odd one for England as well. To get into the cricket eleven, you had to have some talent. In the early years at secondary school each age group only had one team so I was never selected. I occasionally went to practice and bowled at the players who were in the team but I never got a game. It was dispiriting and without encouragement I never practised my batting, and as we got older and bigger and boys got faster I became less and less inclined to go into a net and possibly have my head knocked off. I only got to play when we reached the sixth form and there was a first eleven and a second eleven. I batted at number eleven for the second team.

With my Gray-Nicolls bat, chosen because it looked good on the television and I could lift it, unlike the massive Duncan Fearnley bats of the era, I had two innings in my whole school career. During the first one I was out for nought at Blackpool. In the second, in Bradford, I scored eighteen not out. That innings included three fours all hoiked over the leg side. Maybe it is just in Ben's genes, but I never saw it that way of course. If I had thought that he was performing in such a way because of genetics, I might have left him alone. Instead, I chipped away at him. And not only did I chip away at him in that net session to try to improve his batting, but to my shame I also chipped away at him before and after games too.

The car is a dangerous place both pre- and post-match for parent and child. Athletes often talk about a clear mind helping them succeed in a race or a game, that their ability to cut out all the background noise and chatter so they can simply focus on what lies ahead can be the difference between victory and defeat. Our conversations would leave Ben's mind about as clear as the passenger-side footwell or the side pocket in the rear passenger door.

Strapping him into his seat, I would notice a half-eaten banana in the pocket, although it was close to being taken to forensics so that it could be identified as a banana. Holding this blackened mush with a hint of a yellow between the tips of my thumb and forefinger as if it could explode at any second, I would immediately launch into one.

'Why can't you take your rubbish out? Seriously, how long has this been here? It's disgusting. You are not an animal are you? It is not that hard is it to take your food out of the car when you get out too?' Giving him no chance to answer any of the questions, I would stomp off in search of the correct recycling bin, only then noticing that a half-eaten Harvest Crunch (our attempt at health food with the kids) was stuck to the bottom of the banana/mush.

'And there was a biscuit stuck to that banana as well,' I continued, slamming the car door and starting the engine.

'It was a Harvest Crunch,' came the little voice from behind.

'Well, that isn't the point is it?' I said, thinking if he was as accurate with his bowling today as he was in identifying half-rotting snacks he'd take a few wickets. 'And it was half eaten, just like the banana. At least I think it was a banana. If it had been chocolate, there would have been nothing rotting at all. You would have eaten the lot. You have got to eat the healthy stuff, and all of it not just half of it.'

'OK. Sorry,' he mumbled back and we would continue in silence for a while. The banal arguments, or maybe that should be my frustrations over banal things, would pepper our car journeys. They still do and now there are more, because it isn't just Ben that I have these altercations with, they are with Jessie as well. Trips to their sporting activities are peppered with disagreements over absolutely nothing. From rotting food to . . .

forgetting part of their kit, mainly Ben this one . . .

'How could you not check your bag to see if you had your bat with you? Again, it's not hard is it?'

'Sorry, I thought Mum had put it in.'

'Mum isn't going out to bat for you is she? She shouldn't have to do everything.'

to me forgetting something they needed, mainly Jessie this one . . .

'Have you got my form for this gym competition, Dad?'

'What form?'

'The form I need to hand in when I get there.'

'I didn't know you needed a form. Has Mum not put it in your bag?'

'No. She said you had to pick it up off the table in the hall before we left.'

'Well why didn't she tell me that? It would have been a lot easier if she had just packed it.'

(And yes I can see the irony when it's written in black and white!)

to arguments about the state of the seats . . .

'Why are there footprints on the backs of the front seats and on the backs of the headrests?'

'I was doing stretches on the way to gym practice last week, Daddy.'

'In muddy boots?'

'Yes.'

'Why?'

'Because it had been raining.'

'Not why were they muddy. Why were you doing stretches?'

'To get ready for the session.'

'Yes, but you warm up there.'

'I wanted to warm up for the warm up.'

Just like Ben, who would practise bowling anytime and any-where, Jess was doing cartwheels, handstands and it would appear stretches at any given opportunity.

Anyway, interspersed with these nonsense arguments would be discussions about the sport that they were about to do. They probably just wanted to listen to the radio but I felt I had to ask them questions.

'How are you feeling? Who are you playing/swimming/com-peting against? Try to remember to mark your run up properly/ concentrate on getting that dive right at the start/don't go too fast on your dance routine and get ahead of the music.'

They'd nod or reply and then we'd go back to silence. Were they starting to worry? I have no idea though I'm fairly sure I wasn't helping. We'd turn the radio up, I'd ask them what on earth we were listening to and they would invariably tell me it was the number one and so we'd arrive at our destination with them nerv-ous and me feeling middle-aged and out of touch. Before they left the car to join their teammates I'd always end with, 'Good luck and what's the most important thing to do today?' They knew.

'Have fun,' was the reply.

'Have fun,' I reiterated.

When I relayed these car conversations back to a professional footballer recently, I told him I thought I was being ridiculous in talking to them about what they had to do ahead of the event. That I was putting unnecessary pressure on them before they had to go and do their thing. I wasn't embarrassed about the arguments over keeping a tidy car or remembering your kit, although there is maybe a better time and place for those. He saw things differently, however, and I don't think he was just being kind.

'My dad was completely indifferent to my football when I was growing up,' he told me. 'If I had a game, he wouldn't come. We'd sit in the kitchen and he would simply say "there's your money for the bus to the game and back". And I'd take the money and I'd put it in my pocket and I wouldn't get the bus. I would run all the way to the game, using the jog as a kind of warm up. It gave me determination. That determination, that having to do it all myself to get a game of football, that I'll show you, with or without your help feeling, well, would I be where I am today without that? I don't know. But you are showing you care. You are involved in everything they are doing, with transport and watching and the like and that could be equally important.'

There is no right or wrong answer. Could I be indifferent? I don't think so. Should I learn to be indifferent in certain situations? Probably. I should certainly be indifferent in the car home when a whole load of new questions pop up.

No matter which child and no matter which sport, the car journey home will always start in exactly the same way. They are thirsty and they are starving. I have always come armed with a spare water bottle and several snacks. They start slurping and gobbling down whatever I have brought before I have even pulled out of the car park. As I'm thinking *'I'll probably find part of that snack rotting in the glove box in a fortnight's time'*, they ask to phone their mum if she hasn't been watching too.

'It was great, Mummy. I took five wickets/won the backstroke/ scored three/didn't break my neck falling off the beam.'

'Oh that's great, blah blah blah, so proud, blah blah blah, will give you a big hug when you get home.'

There are smiles and 'love yous' all round and as the phone clicks dead there is plenty of family warmth in the car. A good couple of hours about to be rounded off by a dad who just can't help himself.

'You know when you were bowling, Ben?'

'Yes.'

'It seemed to me that you were landing quite a way behind the wicket. Did you measure your run up properly?'

'Yep.'

'Oh. It just seemed that you were quite a way back. That's all.'

'Oh. I don't think I was.'

'Well it looked it to me.'

'But I took five wickets, Dad.'

'I know, but just imagine if you were actually landing on the crease, the ball would have more pace on it and you could have taken even more.'

An understandable silence from my passenger. I was trying to help. He was thinking *'he may be my dad but he has never taken five wickets in one match in his life so who is he to try and give advice?'* Just as Jessie probably thinks *'he may be my dad but he has never had to do a tumble turn in a race in his life so who is he to try and give advice?'* when we have the following conversation.

'Great race, Jessie.'

'Thanks, Dad. I'm really pleased.'

'Good. So am I.'

Pause . . .

'Jessie?'

'Yes.'

'You know when you are doing your tumble turns, do you think you are going a bit too deep when pushing back off the wall?'

'I don't think so, Daddy. No.'

'Oh. OK. It just looks it.'

'Well I'm not.'

'Well maybe you are, just a bit.'

'But I finished second, Daddy.'

'I know, but maybe you would have won if you hadn't been quite so deep.'

These post-event analysis chats have taken a variety of forms, across a variety of sports and have ended up with a child in tears. We have arrived home to be greeted by a bemused mum who couldn't work out why she had an upset son or daughter when they had done so well according to the earlier phone call. Bemusement that turns to anger when she realises who caused the tears.

When the sports mattered to them we would end up analysing performances in the car. Football (you've got to run more), cricket (we've covered), water polo (yes, I know you made some great saves but do you have to go in goal?) for him. Swimming, gymnastics (keep the run going when you approach the vault, don't stop), netball (try to have soft hands to catch the ball) for her. On all other occasions our car journeys would be fun and peaceful. The key for me, I learnt after the Wigan swimming gala, was to be more like that in the car, even when the sports mattered. To give them space, to talk if they wanted to talk, to help if they wanted help. And to not talk shit. It is something I have managed to master in between the car journeys, when I am actually watching them do their thing.

Chapter 14

I am standing on a hill. The grass at my feet is long, above my ankles and interspersed with daisies, dandelions and weeds all fighting for some attention. Stretched out to my left, underneath wisps of cloud in an otherwise clear blue sky are picturesque Pennine villages. Some belong to the red rose and others to the white rose. The M62 motorway cuts a swathe through the greens and browns with the rumbling traffic audible from many miles away. Somewhere down there, there will be a Nora Batty chasing a Compo with her rolling pin and wrinkled stockings. Up to my right, and it is up because there is an imposing gradient on this hill, are my family. My wife on one of several wooden benches with our youngest on a rug at her feet, barely a year old. Our middle child cartwheeling between the benches, oblivious to anything else going on. Our eldest, yards away from them, yards away from me, with a cricket ball in his hand. There are others. His teammates, two batsmen, two umpires. Over on the far side, a crowd. Parents, club members, bar staff who work in the quaint whitewashed clubhouse. A match at Wimbledon plays on the old television in the corner but that has been usurped by the drama on a Pennine hillside. A drama nobody else knows about. A drama nobody else cares about bar the people huddled together at this village cricket ground. The sky may be blue but that does not guarantee warmth. I shiver, but not from the weather. It is a shiver full of nervousness. I look in the direction of my boy. He returns my gaze. I nod. No words, no gestures. Just a simple movement of my head. He does likewise.

He turns. He runs, rhythmically. He gathers speed over the twenty-five paces it takes him to reach the stumps. He gives himself some height and uses his right arm to aid the direction of his delivery. Over comes his left arm and out comes the dull red ball, its shine long since lost. The batsman steps forward, brings his bat round and with all the power he can muster attempts to hit the ball back from whence it came. He misses and the ball goes through to the wicketkeeper. The fielders puff out their cheeks. The bowler puffs out his cheeks. The bowler's dad puffs out his cheeks and turns away with his back to the game and looks out once again at the beautiful scenery below.

I turn around and my son is walking back to his starting mark, tossing the ball between left hand and right hand. I want him to look in my direction, to offer reassurance, but he only has eyes on the ball. His only thought is winning this game for his side. He starts his run again, moving smoothly once more, but instead of his opponent missing this delivery, the ball connects with the bat. The batsmen scamper between the wickets to earn a run for their side, as a fielder runs round to collect the ball and throw it in to the keeper. There are murmurs of encouragement from their supporters on the other side of the ground. The scoreboard to my left clicks over and adds one to the total. Yorkshire, the mighty Yorkshire, need ten to win off the last four balls.

This time on his walk back he turns to look. I put my thumb up and nod once more but remain silent. He puts his thumb up and smiles. There is no need for any other communication. He knows I am there for him. He also knows what he needs to do. He grimaces as he begins his third approach. Even from the boundary ropes, I can see the determination on his face. This is his battle. This is his game to win for his county, Cheshire, and he is relishing the responsibility. As he releases the ball, I can see he is trying something different. He devours the sport on television and watches the variety of balls that the professional bowlers try in these situations. He is not a professional though. He is only just twelve. He has tried a 'slower ball', in the hope that the batsman cannot spot it and hurries through his stroke before the ball has reached him. This batsman is good though. He has hit a century in this game and is as determined to win this match for his team as Ben is to win it for his. The ball doesn't leave his left hand properly. It is slower but not well directed. It doesn't bounce until it hits the whitewashed walls of the clubhouse. The centurion has dispatched the ball off his pads, with a smoothness and sureness of stroke that belies his years, and the six is greeted with more than just murmurs from his supporters. There are cheers and the warmth of the applause would be welcomed by many, as the temperature has dropped markedly.

My son has also dropped, on to his haunches and nearly on to his knees, just halfway down the wicket. The other batsman evades him as he goes to embrace his teammate just a matter of inches from this devastated bowler. As he raises himself back to his full height, I realise I have inadvertently copied him and I am also on my haunches, picking at the flora between my ankles. My stomach flips, a mixture of nerves and sadness overwhelming it. I know how much this is going to hurt him. I can see him using the sleeve of the white Lycra skin he wears under his short-sleeved cricket shirt to wipe his nose. I cannot be certain, but I am guessing there are tears welling in his eyes. He is probably trying to blink them away as he once more looks at me. I am upright too and my thumb comes up once again and I smile. Nothing comes back this time. Nothing.

My daughter has stopped cartwheeling and has joined her mum on the bench. Whether he had tears or not, I can feel them in my eyes. Not tears because they might lose the game, but tears of pride that he was prepared to put himself through this. Tears that seem to come more readily than they ever did before I had children. Four to win. Three balls in which to get them. They only needed the first of them. Time doesn't stand still in moments like this, that only happens in drama. Everything became more chaotic and more high speed, in complete contrast to the peaceful village life that enveloped this cricketing hillside.

As Ben lay on the floor, the Yorkshire batsmen pumped the air. Supporters on the far side high-fived each other and the rest of the team prepared to come on to the field to congratulate their victorious duo. I didn't move. I observed. I could see my wife, desperate to get off the bench and go and console her son, her mothering instincts kicking in. I motioned for her to stay put because being hit for a six and a four would be nowhere near as embarrassing as being cuddled by your mum in the middle of a cricket pitch. Fortunately for Ben, his teammates rallied round. They picked him up, they consoled him and they took him off the pitch and made sure he was in the line as all the players of Cheshire and Yorkshire shook hands and congratulated each other on what had been a great game of cricket. As I joined in the applause, I realised I hadn't moved. I was still standing where I had been for the whole of his final over. Away from the crowds, away from the coaches and away from my family in blissful, until the final couple of balls, solitude.

From the moment the ball had crossed the boundary rope for the final time, Ben hadn't looked in my direction and now, as he trudged towards the dressing room, I wondered if that mass of mousey brown hair would turn back and allow me to see his face. I started to walk towards my family, willing him to turn around. I had my thumb up ready in case he did. He just kept walking.

We packed up, both parents feeling for their son, both daughters occupying themselves. We walked back to the car, taking one last look at the beautiful scenery. He would be in the changing room for a while as they were debriefed by the coach and then tried to get all their things together, so once the girls were strapped in and the bags in the boot, I went back to wait for him. All of the Yorkshire side were out first and there were nods of appreciation and murmurs of 'well played' as they filed past spectators and parents. The Cheshire players came out in dribs and drabs. Ben wasn't the first and he wasn't the last out of the dressing room. Head bowed, his purple, black and yellow county tie loosely knotted, he was dragging his massive cricket bag along the gravel path, scattering stones as he went. There was the occasional kick of frustration from his black shoes. Should I go and help him, should I console him then and there or should I hang back and wait for him to reach me? I chose the latter. He looked up as he got close and there was a resigned smile on his face. I took his bag off him and dragged it myself and we headed around the clubhouse to the car. There were still plenty of people around so it wasn't the place for a hug.

We walked out on to the road where the car was parked and I popped the boot and heaved his giant bag in there. As it gently closed behind me, we walked to the door behind the driver's seat.

I hugged him. Nobody could see bar his sisters and his mum. I let him go, opened the door and he clambered in. Immediately I could hear Jessie say, 'Well played, Ben, well played.'

We drove off and I looked in the rear-view mirror. He was looking out of the window, lip-synching to whatever was playing on the radio.

'Ben?'

'Yes, Dad?'

'Well played son. I'm so proud, we are so proud, of you volunteering for that final over. It takes a lot of guts that.'

'Thanks, Dad.'

Nobody said anything for a few seconds.

'Dad?'

'Yes?'

'I'm starving.'

And off we drove in search of food that wasn't healthy, saying nothing more about a day that had mattered so much to him and yet had ended in disappointment.

I was learning.

Chapter 15

'He's just like you, you know.'

'What?'

'Ben. He's just like you. Well not like you are now but just like you were when you were his age. It is basically just like watching you all over again.'

'No, it's not. I didn't wear gloves for a start. And I could head a ball.'

'No, you couldn't. Admittedly you didn't wear gloves, but you *attempted* to head the ball in a similar way to how he does. And you lolloped around like that as well.'

And at that my dad maybe had a point. I did lollop and my son certainly lolloped too. There is no greater joy in life than watching your child enjoying playing sport. There is no greater disappointment than realising that they have inherited your pace.

My dad was lucky that I was talking to him; not because I didn't like him or because I objected to his comparisons or because he would mention the likeness approximately once a month but because I don't like to talk to anyone while watching my children. I discovered during my year as a coach that one of the biggest advantages of being on the opposite side of the pitch to the parents was the solitude. It gave me the space to think, the space to enjoy and the space to concentrate without listening to the nonsense coming from the other side. The only time I would hear the nonsense was when it was barked out and as you know we had to try to minimise the nonsense coming from our own footballing parents.

Having run Harrow St Mary's for a year, on moving back North I found myself both missing being a coach and at the same time relieved to no longer be a coach when I rejoined the parental ranks. Strictly speaking, however, it would be stretching it to say that I joined the ranks. I ended up standing near them but never in the thick of it. It was hard not to think *'would I be making that substitution at this point?'* or *'surely the coach needs to encourage the boys to get it wide rather than play it down the middle?'* Of course I never said anything because I believed it wasn't my place to; other parents, however, felt differently. They didn't make comments so that the coach could hear, they saved their louder volume settings to encourage or berate their own children or the opposition, but in quiet moments they would discuss how the coach was performing. Was this what the parents of my team had been doing? When I thought they were being a wonderful bunch and really supportive and buying in to everything, were they whispering criticisms to each other? I have no idea. Probably, because it happens everywhere and in every sport.

For a variety of reasons we have changed Ben's football club three times in the five years that we have been up North. I have heard similar discussions at all three of them. Parents at cricket matches, both at club and county level, discuss where the coach is going right or going wrong, and parents at gymnastics huddle outside the room after a session to query why their little darling only 'got three goes on the vault the whole time they were there and yet their "rival" in another group got ten goes'. I've watched them peer over a swimming balcony muttering to each other that their children should be moved into a faster, better-quality lane or grouped behind a fence at netball saying their daughters should play at Centre so they are in the thick of it, rather than standing at Goal Defence, freezing and hardly touching the ball. I find myself observing and wondering whether they would do the same thing if they observed their children at school. Would they stand at the back of the maths lesson wondering why the teacher only went to their child to answer two multiplication questions when they went to a different child for five questions, or sit in at a science class and be annoyed that their child didn't get a go on the Bunsen burner and was just writing the results of the experiment down? Even on the touchline at a children's sporting event there is paralysis by analysis.

That first football season back, I managed to remain in the throng of parents for maybe six months but I found it hard. Ben was also finding it hard, settling in to a new team, a team that was established from the previous season. They used him in a variety of positions – I'm not sure they ever worked out his strengths and weaknesses – and if he was not having a great game I felt like the eyes of other dads were boring into me. I could have sworn that I heard the odd tut or the odd expletive mumbled under their breath. In that six months I immediately went back to being protective of him and trying not to allow my frustration, mainly with the other parents and not with my son, to come through on the touchline. However, increasingly, after every game we would have *those* conversations in the car on the way home.

'Why don't you get involved more? Maybe you should run more? Do you want me to go to the park with you and do some tackling? Stop pulling your sleeves over your hands, because it looks like you are cold and you don't want to be there.'

'I *am* cold.'

'And do you want to be there?'

'Yes, of course I do.'

'Because if you don't then we can stop. You don't have to play football here. You don't have to play football full stop. Maybe we should just call it a day?'

'No, Dad.' He would be firm and loud and at this point. 'I want to play. I do, I really do.'

'Well maybe you should look like it then, Ben.'

It was before I saw the light about car conversations and real-ised that these chats were doing more harm than good. He now had a kind of threat hanging over him. If you don't look like you are going to enjoy it then I will stop you playing. Well that was hardly going to relax him and put him in the right frame of mind for the next game, was it? I knew he was a decent player so was I frustrated because he wasn't realising his potential or was I frus-trated because I could sense the disapproval of some of the par-ents around? If I am honest, it was the latter. I was more worried about what other people were thinking of him, and to a lesser extent me, than I was about him just enjoying his football.

Halfway through that season, the team were invited to play at a Premier League club's academy. They were going to take on a side who were a year younger than them. The game took place indoors on a cold winter's evening where even though we were under a roof we could see our breath as we spoke to each other. All the boys in our team had at least one of their parents there to watch them and there were plenty of parents from the academy side of things as well. Plenty of 'support'. The academy had enough boys to field two teams so that is exactly what they did. The game would be split into four quarters with one team playing quarters one and three and the other playing two and four. Our team had three substitutes, with the coach able to rotate his players at will. Needless to say, by quarter four our lot were knackered as they took on one of the best sides in the whole of the Manchester area. That final quarter had been preceded by three others that had witnessed plenty of noise, plenty of shouting and plenty of aggression. None of it coming from the players.

The whole concept of being a team went out of the window in that sports hall. It turned into every boy for himself and every parent for himself or herself. Pass it to a teammate in space? No chance. Try to dribble past seven members of the opposition so that the Premier League club might think you are the next Lionel Messi? Definitely. Lose the ball and then get a rollicking from a parent desperate for you to get selected? That's a given.

'Take him on son. That's it, go past him and the next one. Come on,' would come the shout, and it *was* a shout, properly barked by a dad at his kid.

The boy would lose it.

'Oh, come on son. You can do better than that. You can beat men in your sleep. Don't forget your step over. That always works.' The dad would be berating his son, while at the same time hoping the academy coaches were hearing about what he could do normally, when he wasn't under pressure. The pressure put on, of course, by the dad.

Every time a child made a mistake you could feel the tension rise, and not just from our side. Even though the opposition boys were already in a development squad they were still competing against each other to progress through the age groups. And why do a lot of people want them to progress, want them to be professional footballers? Because of the money, because of the untold riches that would come from reaching the very top. Could what would happen in this freezing cold dome be a meal ticket? No, it couldn't, but the atmosphere that night gave the impression that some thought it could. Some would criticise other boys in the team for not passing to their own child, they would criticise their own child as well for not doing something right, and when things did go to plan it felt like a competition as to who could shout their own son's name the loudest in case anybody was making a note of who was doing well. They might throw in their son's surname as well, just to add extra clarification. Bizarrely, Ben scored the first goal of the whole match. If I hadn't passed out with surprise, I could have done something similar.

'Good goal, Ben. Good goal Ben Chapman. Good goal Ben Chapman who lives at such and such an address and if you want to get in touch with me after the game to sign him up then you can ring me on . . .' Instead I was shocked into silence and just gave him a big grin.

We were behind barriers at this game; proper wooden boards, not just a ribbon on some poles. You go up in the world when you arrive at a Premier League academy. As the game drifted on, the noise increased and tempers progressively frayed, I was subconsciously moving further and further away from the barriers until I was quite far from the madding crowd. In my relative isolation, I relaxed and enjoyed watching Ben lollop around, sometimes doing something good and sometimes making a right Horlicks of it. No eyes bored into me and I couldn't hear any tuts, mainly because the other parents didn't know I had stepped away from them and I was out of earshot, but also because it suited them more for my son to make mistakes. If he made mistakes there was less chance of him being picked and perhaps more chance for their own flesh and blood.

As far as I am aware, nobody was picked up from that game. The boys would constantly be told in the weeks that followed that there might be a scout coming to watch from such and such a club. That story does the rounds often, actually. Go to a tournament and you are told that loads of clubs will be scouting it. In the seasons that followed, we were forewarned that a scout would be in attendance at a lot of games. All I can say is that these scouts must be very well camouflaged or are very good at hiding up trees because I have never ever met one at a game of youth football and yet it is amazing how many kids have supposedly been scouted and offered trials. It only seems to happen in football. I have yet to be at a gymnastics competition or a swimming gala where a rumour has swept round that scouts from the big local gym or swimming club have been in among us, ready to sign up a prodigy. And yet when we lived down South our team was supposedly scouted by everyone from Arsenal to Watford and Spurs to Brentford and since being back North, City, United, Bury, Everton, Oldham, you name them, they've all been to watch Ben's teams play.

He had a friend who was actually taken on by one of the Southern-based Premier League clubs. Well, when I say taken on, they wanted to 'have a look at him' for a few weeks. He would duly turn up to their training sessions, dropped off by his mum and dad and picked up by them afterwards. They didn't stay to watch, they weren't allowed to. He hadn't yet reached an age with double figures, but like so many young boys he had huge dreams of becoming a professional footballer and so for a Premier League club to be interested in him, well, this was a sign for him that his dream might actually happen. After six weeks of battling the London traffic for his mum and dad, and for him six weeks battling against other children, late nights, missed homework and plenty of daydreams, the club gave him a letter at the end of one of the sessions. The letter was placed in an envelope and the envelope was addressed to him. He gathered his bits together, no doubt leaving something behind as he was a nine-year-old boy after all, and with his bag over his shoulder he opened the envelope as he made his way out of the building. As he read the letter he discovered that his dreams would have to be put on hold. The club would not be keeping him on. As his mum walked over to collect him she was confronted by her son in tears, thinking his world had come crashing down.

As she told me later: 'Why couldn't they have addressed the letter to us, his parents? We have no problem with them not wanting to keep him on, we didn't expect them to if we are being honest, but if we had opened the letter first then at least we could have managed his disappointment and dealt with it in a sympathetic way rather than him just seeing it in stark black and white.'

The cut-throat, cold-hearted world of professional sport, eh? Children, and they are only children, are judged, analysed and discarded. But it's not just in that trial environment at a professional club that they are scrutinised, it is every single time they step on to a pitch or dive into a pool. Not only by their coaches, because that is part of their job, but by the parents too.

I had enjoyed stepping away from the throng at Ben's game against the academy side. Well, 'enjoyed' is not the right word; 'becalmed' might be better. I had felt becalmed, standing on my own, away from some of the less audible comments. Yes, I could still hear plenty but not the mutterings of discontent. I left there thinking this was going to be a good tactic going forward. I wasn't going to stand with any group any more. I was going to stand on my own, away from everybody, at any sporting event my children were at. And that is what I've done.

Most parents at football matches congregate around the half-way line: I now stand down towards one corner depending on what position my son is playing. The majority of parents at the cricket congregate around a clubhouse or a pavilion: I tend to sit or stand on the opposite side of the ground to the facilities. At swimming galas, most parents try to get as close to the finish line as possible, I just take one of the seats in the viewing gallery in line with the middle of the pool because they seem to be the least popular. At gymnastics competitions, I either find a spare seat and hope nobody sits next to me or I stand at the back, where I can move if someone tries to talk to me. My wife thinks I do this because I am a 'grumpy arse'. Other parents probably think I do this because I am a 'grumpy arse' and there is a good case to suggest that at times I am a 'grumpy arse'. If I'm honest, I know I can be. But it also gives me peace of mind and keeps me away from a lot of the nonsense and a lot of the anger.

The anger is there every single week, in football more than the other sports. Anger directed at the referee, at the boys, at other parents, sometimes between parents supposedly on the same side, and at the coaches. Nobody, it would appear, is immune from the vitriol, and arguably nobody in a game of kids' football deserves it, not even the referees.

After those early years, you are allocated qualified referees for your games. You can't just give the job to a well-meaning dad to stop him having a go at his own son! Judging by the referees Ben's teams have had over the years, I would guess that most of the officials they get are recently qualified as well. This is not to cast aspersions on their abilities, but the majority of them are only a few years older than the boys themselves. Such a situation can be applauded, because in my experience of amateur adult football, our referees were always a lot closer to the grave than the cradle. In a footballing sense they were always close to the centre circle, because they weren't particularly mobile. In the kids' games, these refs are mobile. They are often acne-ridden, self-conscious and taking their first steps in their chosen area of the sport. At times they appear to surprise themselves when they blow their whistle to make a decision. Just like the players, they need support and encouragement. They don't get it.

'How can you give that? How can you give that?'

A referee in one of our games, ginger-haired and flushed of face, had awarded the opposition a goal. He had adjudged that the ball had crossed the line despite our goalkeeper's best efforts to keep it out.

'He kept it out. We could all see that.' Ben's coach wasn't letting this go. 'That's pathetic ref. Pathetic.'

The referee's face flushed: even more, I would guess, from the attention than from anger. He didn't look the angry sort.

'You are a disgrace. A disgrace.' Our coach continued to go up and down the touchline, belittling the referee. As well as being a coach, he was a successful businessman who should have known better. He should have known better on account of the fact that he was in his forties, and he should have known better because he was a sports enthusiast who cared. His behaviour encouraged that of some of our own parents. Nothing that was said was too aggressive, just the odd comment when the ref was in earshot; maybe something sarcastic to undermine him and make the other dads roar with laughter. Standing by the corner flag, I heard some of the comments; others were a bit too quiet or sly.

'About time you gave us something, ref,' when he blew for a free kick in our favour. 'You sure that didn't cross the line?' when their keeper made a save, several yards off his line. And if the coach was doing it and the parents were doing it then some of the boys might as well try it as well. Of course, if they did, the ref would then have a word with them, provoking more objections from the sidelines. Such is the way of the world that we lost that game by the odd goal. The coach was under the impression that in a 5–4 defeat the one that he thought hadn't crossed the line was the one that had made the difference. He even went to talk to the referee at the end of the game.

My personal opinion, stood in serene isolation, was that he had had a good game. He had been fair, good with the kids and hadn't been intimidated by all the stick. As he left the pitch, I shook his hand.

'Good game. Well reffed.'

'Thanks,' he mumbled, eyes down. He kept on walking. As I turned to follow him, he was greeted by a man a few years older than me, who had been standing in my vicinity for the whole match. The man put his arm around the referee's shoulder. A consoling gesture as they walked towards the car park. The referee just shook his head. They reached the car in conversation, with the man's arm rubbing the boy's back. He was obviously upset. The ref jumped into the passenger seat and the man who had just watched his son get constant stick and abuse for the last hour got in beside him and prepared to drive his boy home. A miserable morning completed. A morning watching his own flesh and blood doing something he enjoyed, because people do enjoy refereeing, while getting hammered by middle-aged men for doing it.

But the parents don't hammer officials in the other sports I attend. In every swimming gala I have attended since Wigan, and including Wigan, I have watched competitors being disqualified. It has happened to my own daughter. They might not have turned correctly or touched the wall properly, or else they used the wrong kick. Often, you never find out why; you just find out when it is announced over the loudspeaker.

'First was so and so, second this person, third that person and swimmer X from this club was disqualified.'

At no point have I then seen a disgruntled parent stand up in the balcony and berate the officials down below. More often than not there is a shrug, a resigned acceptance that their child must have done something wrong, and then back to talking to the person next to them. Or in my case, back to my book and hoping nobody sits next to me.

At gymnastics competitions, everything is subjective. The judges give marks to the children for their routines or vaults or performances. The judges also belong to the clubs that are competing, so if somebody wanted to they could easily throw accusations of favouritism or bias when the results are read out. Again though, I have never seen a parent storm the podium – yes, they actually have a podium at these things – to complain about a result. It is accepted, everybody is applauded and everybody moves on.

By the time the medals are given out in gymnastics I don't have the strength to complain even if I wanted to. Despite my preference for solitude, I find it doesn't particularly help me. I end each one feeling mentally and physically drained. They are gruelling. They are not quick things. I haven't been at one that has lasted less than three hours and just like a swimming gala I have to pay for the privilege. Once again, I pay three pounds to watch my daughter and a hundred like her do a forward roll. Jessie had already been to a couple of competitions with her mum by the time I went to my first one with her. She was already an expert, so I knew I had to pay, where she had to be at what time and where

I should sit to get the best view of her. Her mum was away but had left all the necessary kit out for her and packed her bag. All I had to do was take her, watch her and come back with her. There was one thing, however, that I had not been forewarned about. Something that I was not ready for then and will never be ready for again. Something that was to test every bone in my body and every ounce of patience I had.

Chapter 16

We paid. We walked in. We found a seat. We put her bag under my seat. She saw some of her friends. She waved. They waved back. She was about to run off and join them. She stopped. She looked at me.

'Daddy?'

'Go on. They are all over there. Just join them. Don't worry about me, I'll be fine.'

'No, Daddy. I can't go yet.'

'Yes, you can, it's fine. I'll keep your stuff here. You go and warm up.'

She didn't move. With her eyes fixed on mine she uttered the words that sent a chill down my spine. 'Daddy. You need to do my hair.'

Not only was there a chill down my spine, I also had a feeling of being punched in the gut.

'What?' This was not said with annoyance or in a loud voice, but in a soft, querying, almost pleading, hoping that she hadn't said what I thought she had said, kind of way.

'You need to do my hair,' she reiterated, as she opened up the side pocket of her gym bag to reveal what to her was a gleaming array of brushes, bobbles, pins and clips and to me was a torture chamber. My daughter sat down on the adjoining seat, put the bag on her lap and turned her back and in doing so presented her thick mass of naturally curly hair to me. I picked the brush out of the pocket because that was one of the few things in there I knew how to use. I started brushing. It was a good start. I kept brushing and brushing, although it soon became clear she was expecting her hair to have more than just the knots taken out.

'What are you going to do with it, Daddy?'

'Well, what would you like me to do with it, Jessie?' I replied and at the same time thinking *'please just say "keep brushing it, keep brushing it".'*

'Well, I'd like it in a bun please.'

Now that wasn't the worst option. It wasn't the best, that would probably have been a ponytail, but she could have said plaits or bunches which I would have found infinitely harder to do than a bun.

'No problem. We'll give that a go.'

We had always told the kids that if they tried their best we could never be angry with them and so I had to follow my own advice. Unfortunately it didn't work the other way round. I did try my best and she was still somewhat unimpressed with me. In my head, a bun was a simple matter of scrunching up all her hair to make a mound on top of her head, stick some clips in it, a quick wazz of hairspray round it and job done. That was in *my* head. In *her* head it looked like I had scrunched up her hair to make a mound, stuck some clips in it and then wazzed a lot of hairspray on it. She was not best pleased. The 'mound' was not best balanced. I could feel eyes burning into me from mothers of other competitors who were completing their own works of art on their own daughters' heads in the vicinity; they reflected disgust at my incompetence, sympathy for my daughter. But they were not going to offer to help as she was in competition with their own flesh and blood.

Off she went to join her teammates, easy for me to spot because her hair stood out and indeed stood up from all the rest. Within minutes she was back with me, one of her coaches in tow, who was wearing either a grimace or a sympathetic smile. It was difficult to tell. She took charge of the hair situation and within minutes they were back off to the mats, a bun perfectly formed on my daughter's small head.

As with a swimming gala I had a programme and as with a swimming gala it was going to be a long morning. There were over sixty children at this competition representing four different clubs. They were separated into different age groups and abilities and would be performing in two different disciplines. They would each get two attempts at the vault and they would also perform a short floor routine set to music. Just as at the swimming, the experienced parents had claimed the best seats where they would find it easy to watch both sections. I was craning my neck from towards the back of the hall to even see one.

Concentration is the key at these things. Plenty of focus is required along with stamina and you need to listen. What the children need I have no idea but those are the qualities required to be a good spectator. Every gymnast is announced to the crowd and they have to do a little step forward and raise their arms in the air as they do so. They 'present' is the technical term and in return they get applause and cheers from the crowd, the coaches and the other gymnasts. Jessie's group were allocated the vault first. She was one of around twenty children in that batch doing that discipline. It is not easy to keep your interest up when watching child after child run, vault and then land. Your mind starts to drift, you start reading the paper and as each child is not announced it is very easy to miss your own kid's turn; which I did. I looked up from the paper to see her walking back to rejoin the group, having had her first turn. I did our standard sign of putting my thumb up in the hope she thought I had seen it. Her look told me she knew I hadn't. I had to make amends and not miss her second jump, which would be at least half an hour away. Even though I knew I had thirty minutes to do whatever I wanted I couldn't allow myself to be distracted. I had to sit and watch a plethora of children run, vault and land before my own child stepped up again: and the crafty little thing had a look round before she began, just to check that my nose wasn't back in my paper.

With the first round of exercises complete, there then followed a reminder not to take photos (standard) and also not to take photos of the photos the professional photographer was pinning up on the boards at the back for you to buy. We were told that if you were doing that you were breaking some child protection law, though it was more likely you were denting the profits of the professional photographer. With parents suitably admonished, the children all switched positions. Vault went to floor, floor went to vault. She would only have one go at this, as would I, but she would be announced before her routine so I would have some forewarning.

As each girl performed her routine, and each club had the same piece of music, I had to listen to the same song again and again and again. I was aware that gym parents do exactly what football parents do, which is exactly what cricket parents do and that is analyse. They do it in hushed tones so as not to disturb anyone, least of all the gymnast, but the whispers of the ones nearest to me were audible.

'Her toes weren't very straight there.'

'The forward roll went slightly wonky at the end.'

'She struggled to get out of that bridge.'

'Her legs needed to be straighter in that handstand.'

'She's lost her timing, she's way ahead of the music.'

And so it continued, performer after performer, amateur analysis after amateur analysis, which meant yet again, when Jessie stepped up to do her routine, I had that feeling of *'please don't let me hear them analysing my daughter'* rather than *'please let my daughter perform how she wants to.'* I concentrated so hard on what she was doing I didn't hear anything from anybody in the vicinity and as she ended her routine with a smile on her face and a wave at me I assumed it had gone well, because I'll be honest with you I wasn't able to tell a good routine from a poor one. I started to pack up our stuff so that once she had put her tracksuit back on we could make a quick getaway. I was still there an hour later.

I am learning that nothing should be rushed in gymnastics and that includes the medal ceremonies. The competitors first of all have to do a kind of parade whereby they form a long line and walk around the arena to receive the applause of the crowd. They then sit in their club groups and every individual is announced and awarded a medal for competing. There are then medals for every age group. But not one set of medals. There is a gold, silver and bronze medal ceremony for the vault. There is a gold, silver and bronze medal for the floor and then there is a gold, silver and bronze ceremony for the overall scores. We eventually walked out of there with Jessie resembling a middle-aged man going clubbing in the 1970s, with several medals around her neck. She had one silver, two golds and the medal for just competing. She had won the overall gold. As we jumped in the car, I told her that was down to me.

'But you can't even do a handstand, Daddy,' she told me indignantly, as I tried to take credit.

'I know, but you didn't have time to worry about today, did you? There was no time for Billy, Bert and Bob to be in your stomach.' Billy, Bert and Bob are the names we have given to the butterflies in her tummy.

'No, I didn't.'

'And that was because,' I said, warming to my theme, 'I made such a mess of your hair and you were laughing, kind of, at how useless I was and so you didn't have time to worry and that helped you.'

'No, I won the medals because they thought I was the best.'

It was difficult to argue with that. Being the best at sport is not something that has been passed down the Chapman family tree, and yet I find myself in situations where my children are regularly bringing home medals and certificates. Obviously there are several token ones in there for participation, being polite, not getting exasperated at your dad's attempts at doing your hair, but there were also ones for genuine achievement. For winning races, winning competitions, player of the year, most goals or most wickets. We keep having to put up new shelves in their rooms for new trophies. For a man who had only books on his shelves, bar the Cub of the Month trophy I won when I was eight, this is hard to fathom. It also, if I'm honest, provokes the odd pang of jealousy.

Chapter 17

The sporting genes must have just skipped a generation. My dad played rugby union to a decent standard and my two eldest children have genuine designs to make it at a high sporting level. I was mired in sporting mediocrity and even that might be being slightly generous. Of course I do not blame it on my genes. Even in middle age, I still tell my parents that if they hadn't been so strict and had allowed me to play football for five hours per night rather than having to do my maths or English homework, then I could have been a professional footballer. I will more than likely still be proffering that theory into old age.

By the time I was in secondary school my parents would have known that I wasn't going to be a professional sportsman. Not being picked for the A team in either football or cricket was probably quite a big clue. If there were already so many lads ahead of me at school, imagine what it would be like in the rest of Greater Manchester. When I didn't make the football team at school, they suggested I give rugby a go. I could have sworn I saw my dad smirk when I told him. After one game, where I constantly seemed to find myself at the bottom of a pile of bodies and even when I was vertical rather than horizontal had no idea whether I should be throwing the ball or kicking it, I left it well alone. I went back to football and played some games for the B team in that first year. None of them memorable.

I was a year young for that age group so it meant that the following season I was allowed to remain playing for the Under-12 team rather than move up to the U13 team and I don't know whether the new intake were weaker or whether I had got stronger or more confident, but from then on I was playing A-team football. For six years I played for my school and for six years my dad stood there watching. You could count the number of games he missed on one hand. My mum used to come too for the first couple of years, until I banned her. She had decided to turn up for an afternoon game in early spring dressed in a knee-length quilted coat. Over the top of the coat she had decided to wear a cagoule, presumably thinking her coat wasn't waterproof. She topped off this look with a pair of moon boots, apparently under the impression that three feet of snow could fall during the course of the ninety minutes. This eccentric look was very embarrassing for a thirteen-year-old boy and afterwards I suggested she might want to give footy a miss for a while. The next time she turned up to watch a member of her family play sport was when she came to watch my son and I admit I paid close attention to her when she swung her legs out of the passenger seat to get out of the car, just in case there was a pair of moon boots on the end of them.

There was another reason, bar the sartorial one, for excluding my mum. My stroppy, argumentative nature was becoming more prevalent on the pitch. There were late tackles and disagreements with the opposition and even more disagreements with the referee. I had even started to swear. Shocking I know. And for my mum it would have been worse. Even to this very day, I don't think she has ever heard me swear. She has had one unfortunate conversation about blow jobs when she caught Ben watching the movie *Ted* while she was babysitting, but aside from that I have always respected the fact that she doesn't like swearing and therefore I don't do it around her. So for all those years my dad traipsed around the North West, whether it be rain, wind or shine, most of the time on his own, while I performed like a stroppy adolescent. He didn't even see me score until the final season I played for the school. This wasn't because I had scored on those very odd occasions he hadn't been able to make it. It was because I had never put the ball in the back of the net for the school. Seventeen years I had been on the earth, for roughly nine of them I had been in football teams, for six of them I had played for this school and through all of them I had never scored a goal. It all changed on the last Saturday in November in 1990. Even though it is over twenty years ago, I can be specific about the date, because as well as my goal drought ending I passed my driving test and my now wife asked me out. As I said in my groom's speech, 'let me tell you about how the most important of those three events came about'.

We were playing our biggest local rivals. We had played them twice a year, every year throughout our school career and this was going to be our final ever home game against them. In every one of those games, I had gone up against the same striker. A lad with the surname Pinkerton. Taller than me, stronger than me and more cumbersome than me. His teammates constantly referred to him as 'Pinky', which was hilarious to us, the opposition, as we made our way through the age groups. His dad, just like mine, was present at every single game we played against them. Always dressed in a bobble hat and scarf in the school's colours, he would have matched my mum for catwalk elegance if I hadn't banned her. The two would often stand in the same area, sometimes side by side, no doubt laughing at the stupidity of their sons as they tried to take lumps out of each other.

There was nothing special about this game; a typical wet, cold, grey Mancunian morning, some seventeen-year-old lads laughing at 'Pinky' being shouted across the pristine, big pitch we used for our home games, my dad standing in proximity to the bobble-hatted one. Nothing special I should say until, with just moments left in the game and us 2–1 down to our big rivals, the ball came to me. I was on the halfway line with space in front of me. I took a touch, then another and another. I couldn't get the bloody thing under control. By the time I had I was ten to fifteen yards inside the opponents' half. Let's call it ten for dramatic effect. My team-mates were screaming for me to pass to them, knowing that if I didn't I would lose possession. I looked up. I ignored the cries for the ball, took one final touch and then hammered the ball towards goal. From forty yards (if you are going on the measurement of only being ten yards inside their half for dramatic effect). I have no idea how but I caught it just right. It flew towards the goal. Their keeper had been off his line and he started to backpedal. For a couple of seconds, as he started to go backwards and the ball arced towards his net, I started to think *Bloody hell I could have scored here, I could have scored here. That's going in.* That quickly turned to *Bloody hell, I have scored* as the ball went into the roof of the net over the keeper's outstretched fingers. I didn't know what to do. I had never had to celebrate before and fortunately my decision was taken for me as my surprised teammates launched themselves on me. I am told that my dad jumped so high when the ball hit the back of the net that he nearly had to be rescued from one of the trees that lined that pitch. There was laughter followed by grunts and howls of surprise from all the lads on top of me and from underneath all my teammates' bodies I could just make my dad out. He was definitely on terra firma and he was shaking the outstretched hand of Pinky's dad.

I thought his joy was slightly over the top: after all, it was me who had scored the wonder goal, me who had broken my duck, me who was taking the glory. It was only when I had my own children that I understood his sheer elation. We freeze on touchlines, we sweat on balconies, we struggle with hair clips just to experience those moments. Those moments when your child does something special; either special for them individually or special for the team they are playing in; those moments when they turn and look at you and just beam with joy. Those moments when they are mobbed by overjoyed teammates and those moments when they feel they have contributed. When they happen, the wet, the mud, the journeys, the tantrums, the arguments and the nerves are all worth it. When they touch the wall first in a swimming race and turn around looking for you, beaming, as they struggle to remove their goggles; when they score the winning penalty in a shootout in a tournament to go through to the next round and are jumped on by their teammates; when they finish the floor routine in front of you and let out a huge sigh of relief because it has gone to plan; when they surprise themselves and you by somehow scoring with a header; when they score their first ever point in netball and jump up and down on the spot as the ball trickles through the net. All of these moments make it worth it. And when you are not there, it hurts. Family life and work life make it nigh on impossible to be at every single thing your child does, but I feel a tremendous guilt when I know I can't watch them. It is worsened if they have done something really well in my absence, knowing that they might have turned round to smile or put their thumbs up and then realised that I wasn't there to share their joy.

I always want them to do well, but when I get the call from an event that I haven't been able to attend then I wonder whether I sometimes find it easier when it hasn't gone as well. If I'm told Ben's team have lost 6–1, or Jessie didn't win her swimming race, is there a part of me that thinks *'well thank goodness I haven't missed something special'*? Yes, I think, there probably is. When I have taken the call to tell me Ben scored a special goal to win a tournament for his school or that Jessie scored her highest ever mark to win the vault competition do I hang up and then beat myself up that I wasn't there to see it? Yes, I definitely do. I am delighted of course that they have done what they have done, but I feel sorry for myself that I wasn't there and I wonder if they wish I had been there to see it too.

My forty-yard thunderbolt for school in that game wasn't special because it was against our local rivals. It wasn't special because I had the last laugh over Pinkerton. It wasn't special because I had never scored before and thought I would never ever score for school. It was special because my dad was there. I had made my dad happy.

Chapter 18

When that ball hit the back of the net from forty yards it was already very clear that I was not going to be a professional sportsman. It had been clear for many years that I was not going to be a professional sportsman, probably from that moment when I was first put in goal. Talent, and in particular pace, were also going to put paid to any ideas I had of that, that's if indeed I had any ideas and I am not sure I did.

If I am saying I wasn't going to be a professional sportsman, what I am in fact saying is I wasn't going to be a professional footballer, because that was all we thought we could be in the sporting world while growing up. We would watch Daley Thompson win Olympic golds, or Duncan Goodhew cut a swathe through the pool or David Gower hit beautiful cover drive after beautiful cover drive, but would we ever think we could emulate them? Not really. The only cycling we knew of was putting our mudguards down on to the tyres of our Grifters to make them sound like motorbikes. We didn't consider it a sport. Watch Bryan Robson eating up the midfield ground or Joe Corrigan pull off another save and think we could be the next big thing for United or City then yes, that could be a dream. We would hear of a mate of a mate who had had a trial at a club so we knew it was possible and we were playing football every day in the playground or on a field behind our houses, so we could get spotted at any time. We weren't on the field trying to pole vault over the small brook that ran through the middle of it in the hope an athletics coach was walking past. We didn't even know athletics coaches existed. Daley Thompson must have just happened. If you had asked me between the ages of nine and twelve what I wanted to be I would have said 'footballer' and done nothing about it. It would have been a dream and nothing more. If you had asked my son since the age of ten what he wanted to be he would have always said 'cricketer'. He doesn't say it and then do nothing about it though. He says it and then expects something to be done about it, or more specifically his parents to do something about it.

The first thing we had to do was not discourage him, although if my early net sessions with him and the cones hadn't discouraged him then I am not sure anything would. We had progressed from there, he had progressed from there and thank goodness for that. When he was asked where he wanted to be in ten years' time he would say 'playing cricket for England'. If you had asked him a year previously he could well have responded with 'Anywhere. Anywhere that doesn't involve me being in a net with my dad and his cones and him thinking he can coach.' He was starting to show a determination and a dedication that I hadn't seen in him before. Certainly not in his football, certainly not in his swimming, which after the first couple of galas had started to tail off and of course not in his schoolwork.

'Come on Ben, you've got English homework to do. You need to read to me for twenty minutes tonight.'

'Oh, do I have to? I can read to myself in bed later and you can just sign my diary and say that I've done it.'

'I can't do that Ben. You have to read to me.' I was trying to be firm but equally in my mind I came back to my age-old argument of 'if only my mum and dad hadn't forced me to do my homework . . .' Plus an evening in the garden playing cricket with my son would be a lot more enjoyable than listening to him stumble his way through *Charlotte's Web* for the next twenty minutes. No, I had to be strong and firm and do what's best for my son.

'OK, let's go and play cricket then,' I said, followed by cheers from him and 'best dad ever' comments, which eased my guilt. Slightly. He could get me out and he knew that he could get me out, as he had proved in the nets when we had moved North and while comfortable(ish) with that notion I didn't know quite how to deal with having a talented sportsman as a son.

Every parent thinks they have the best child in the world and a lot of dads think they have an amazing sporting son on their hands. So many dads when they hold their son for the first time will look at their partners and tell them that this little thing they have created will go on to play football/cricket/rugby for their country. Grandpa will hold him for the first time.

'He'll captain Manchester United/Yorkshire/Leicester Tigers this one.'

It's highly unlikely he'll come in and say 'this one will play the trumpet for the Hallé when he's older. Mark my words.' My father-in-law was a professional musician and even he went down the sporting route when he held Ben for the first time. Whatever you say at that emotional time, you don't really believe it. You might hope for it, but you don't believe it. As I saw Ben's football career develop I knew that I couldn't hope for it.

'You aren't going to be a footballer son.'

'I might be. You never know.'

'No, I do know. You have inherited my pace.'

'No I haven't. I'm quick I am.'

'You aren't. You are really skilful but you are slow.'

'I'm not. I'll race you back to the car.'

And I'd beat him back to it and prove my point, even though he was only eight and my legs were at least twice as long as his.

But with his cricket, it was different. He was developing and developing and becoming very, very good. Not only could I see it with my very own eyes and feel it with my very own knees when cricket balls started ricocheting off them, but the sheer number of wickets he was taking was backing it up and other people were commenting on it as well.

His coach at his club would tell me, 'He's bowling beautifully. The accuracy at his age is remarkable. He's definitely got something.'

'Yes . . . well . . . erm, he's enjoying it, so that's all that matters.'

We don't deal with praise very well as a family. We deal very much in self-deprecation and boasting is not on the agenda, which I realise might seem slightly odd as at the moment I am writing about how wonderful my son is. But rather than concentrate on that, concentrate more on how badly at times I struggle to deal with it. That would make me feel better. Concentrate on my shambolic parenting efforts rather than his ability. Please?

Other dads would talk to me about how well he was playing, that he could maybe play for the county and so on and so forth and rather than welcome their lovely comments I would resort to worrying in my head that what they really thought was that I was a pushy dad. That I was drilling him relentlessly at home so that he could reach these standards. A pushy dad bragging about his amazing son. The dad that other people avoid on the boundary rope so that they don't have to listen to him banging on about how amazing his offspring is. Fortunately they didn't have to avoid me because I was using my solitary watching technique, keeping as far away from other parents as possible, just so that they didn't think I was showing off about Ben.

He was devouring everything to do with the sport. Books, magazines, coaching videos on the internet. The television would more often than not be showing a cricket match when he was in the room. A game between the West Indies and Sri Lanka or a one-dayer between Bangladesh and South Africa. Matches that would get no more than a few thousand watching them on TV in this country and he was one of those few, trying to learn about the game.

It all helped him though because he, along with some of his teammates, was then put forward to district coaching sessions which would lead on to county trials if you were successful. Sport, which throughout our family history had always been a leisure pursuit and nothing more, was starting to get a bit more serious. He was setting himself targets. Targets in the sense of the number of wickets he was wanting to take but also targets relating to who he wanted to play for and by when. He was trying to choose a career path. So we were left with a dilemma shared by many parents, not just those with sporty kids: how much do you encourage and how much do you inject a dose of realism? Obviously you want to encourage as much as possible but with sporty kids that comes at a cost, more so than with non-sporty kids. A non-sporty kid says she wants to be an airline pilot when she grows up, you don't go out and buy her a plane. You probably tell her to study the right subjects at school, maybe go to a few air displays and watch the planes land and take off at an airport. Doctor, policeman, lawyer, nurse; there are few cost implications if that is the career dream of a child. A ten-year-old says he wants to be a doctor, you don't have to buy him a new stethoscope every year. If a child wants to be a footballer or a cricketer then there is new equipment they need every single season, or in my children's case every single season and then again halfway through every season.

'I need some new boots.'

'No, you don't, we only bought you those two months ago.'

'Yes, but they are starting to feel tight.'

'Well they don't look tight and you scored in them last week so they aren't exactly hindering you.' I thought highlighting the positives would throw him off the scent and he would look fondly on his footwear if it was bringing him success.

'Well, my coach says he thinks they are on the tight side and that really I could do with some new ones.' He's playing the 'expert' card early. Bringing in his coach and putting him on his own side makes him think that I will cave in. It's now two v. one.

'Oh he does, does he?' And then I reach for the standard parenting line 'and is he going to pay for them? Does he know how much these boots cost?'

Ben tries to answer, too young at this stage to understand the principle of a rhetorical question, but I cut him off with the second standard parenting technique. 'I never needed more than one pair of boots in a season.' Classic. Always bring it back to our own day. If it was good enough for me thirty years ago then it should be good enough for my son now. Obviously that conveniently ignores the fact that if my dad had used that reasoning I would have been playing in boots as heavy as bricks when I was a child.

'You'll be fine. Your boots will be fine, so just get on with it.'

He'd slope off and before he'd even get out of the room I'd feel guilty.

'Oh, OK. Put them on, let me see.'

He knew he'd got me, even after that one sentence. We'd go through him taking ten minutes to put a boot on just to emphasise how tight they were and then, even though I was thinking the boot wasn't going on easily because he was incompetent rather than it being too small, I'd tell him, 'Go and look on the internet and see what boots you can find.'

'One hundred and eighty quid. One hundred and eighty quid. One hundred,' I paused, 'and eighty' another pause 'quid. Of all the boots on that site you have found a pair that cost one hundred and eighty pounds.'

'Yes, but they mould themselves to your feet, give you more power when you hit the ball . . .', he began, and then he started to reel off all their other 'amazing' qualities as I tried to scan the page for anything cheaper. I came back into his reasons for wanting them as he ended with 'and they are the boots worn by Robin van Persie'.

'They'd have to have been actually worn by van Persie for me to pay that amount for them,' I said, sounding more and more like a stereotypical Northern dad with each sentence. 'You aren't having them. Look there's a pair that look exactly the same but are only forty pounds. Shall we get them?'

'Yeah, but they aren't made of the same material and they don't have this and they don't have that.'

'Can you kick a ball with them?'

'Yes.'

'We'll get them then.'

'OK. Oh, I also need a pair of AstroTurf trainers too, because they're too tight as well. My coach says.'

'Well get the same pair, at the same price, in AstroTurf trainers too.' We were going through four pairs of boots or AstroTurf trainers per season. Often he'd wear his new ones, have an awful game, blame the new boots and then go back to the old ones for a couple of games, which had miraculously become less tight. Once the blisters came, he had to go back to his new ones, unlucky or not.

We always go standard and cheapish for the boots because we go through them so quickly and because in essence, whatever the marketing departments of sportswear manufacturers say, a football boot is there to kick a ball with and that's all that matters. The fact that they have models that cost the earth because they have made them out of hi-tech material they tested on the moon is of no concern to us. What works on the moon might not work for a ten-year-old splashing through puddles and ankle-length grass in South Manchester.

Going with standard and cheapish when it comes to the cricket is less of an option. Safety is the biggest reason why. If I'm buying a helmet for him to bat in, I don't want to consider cheapish because I don't want something at the lower end of the market protecting my son's head. I want it to be encased in something well made and sturdy and, rightly or wrongly, I assume that something which costs more is more likely to have those qualities. To a slightly lesser extent, I use the same theory with gloves and pads and box, again all protective equipment required for a batsman. I don't tend to go as expensive with those because they are only protecting his fingers, his legs and his you know what and none of those are as important as his head. Even his you know what.

He'll ask for a new bat every year, always on the excuse that the one from the previous season is too small and he is usually correct. He did try to change his bat mid-season once because, yet again, he thought it was unlucky. He 'kept missing the ball with it'. I was quite firm in pointing out that it might not be the bat's fault. And all this equipment is carried around in a bag the size of a small bungalow and that needs changing every season for health reasons alone. Fungi, yet to be named by scientists, are growing in a twelve-year-old's cricket bag by the time a summer season draws to an end and no amount of Febreze can disguise the smell. I will gladly lay out the cash to remove a health hazard from my house.

Yet health and safety is probably not the main reason we stump up for his cricket equipment. No pun intended. We do it because it is his passion and we want to support him. Would I feel a sense of guilt if we weren't buying a new bat every season? I probably would. Am I a soft touch? I probably am. I can see how much it means to him though and therefore I don't want to be the one holding him back. It would break my heart in several years' time if he hadn't made it because we hadn't done enough for him, or if he thought we hadn't done enough for him. Of course, it doesn't simply come down to buying equipment: the impact on our time and family life is greater than the impact on my wallet.

We have friends whose daughter is a sensational swimmer. Not just a swimmer who will win races for her club, but a swimmer who competes at national championships and has been to the Olympic trials. She is not yet old enough to drive. Four times a week she trains at five in the morning. That means she has to be in the pool by five in the morning – so she has to leave at four thirty in the morning. As a result, her mum or dad have to be up at four fifteen in the morning. Four times a week. While one takes her, the other grabs an extra couple of hours in bed. They will then get up to prepare breakfast for their daughter and eventually get their son up. They drop their son off to get the bus and drive on to the pool to pick up their daughter, who they then take to school while she eats her prepared breakfast alongside them.

Four times a week. With both kids at school, they go off to their jobs. They are not done there. Along with those four mornings, she does five evening sessions, some in the pool and some in the gym. Again they require transport and food preparation. If you then add in the competitions and club galas at the weekend, it is a seven days a week operation for the girl and the parents. But they can't say no, can they? They can't say 'do you know what, we are so tired that just tomorrow can you miss the five a.m. session? Please?' And the reason they can't say it is because the fear will be burned into their minds that if their daughter missed the Olympics by 0.001 of a second they would always have the thought that they caused her to miss a training session because they wanted one lie-in.

So you end up saying yes to everything.

There's a county training session fifty miles away? No problem, he'll be there.

The session lasts two hours, you say, so I'll have to stay because it's pointless to drive home and then come back? No problem, I'll hang around and watch.

There are no facilities to watch, you say? No problem, I'll just build up my points in Costa by ploughing through a few flat whites and the odd muffin.

They are going to play in a festival in the South West, you say? For four days, you say? It would be great if we could come and support, you say? OK, we'll book a cottage down there and bring the whole family with us and build our summer around that then. Oh, and there are ten other fixtures preceding that, you say? He'll have to miss school for some of them, you say? We need to organise that with the teachers, you say? Leave it with us.

I have interviewed many sportsmen and women over the years, and so many of them thank their parents after a success. I now understand why. If your child has a talent and chooses to give it a really good go then it can take over your own life and your family life. I don't begrudge Ben one single minute of my time as he tries to pursue his dream but as one embattled parent said to me after an early start and a long journey, as they prepared to spend hours watching their child train, 'I do sometimes think, why can't he have just played the violin?'

Ben couldn't have played the violin because there is not a musical bone in his body. I have definitely passed on my musical incompetence to him. There are plenty of cricket bones though. I have definitely not passed on my cricketing incompetence to him. In his first year of trying to make the grade for the county, he fell just short. Remarkably he didn't sulk, even though I have passed on sulky tendencies to him, but instead it just made him more determined. He wanted to play as much cricket as he possibly could. The summer he was rejected he would play at least three games a week. There would be a midweek one, a Friday night one and a Sunday morning one for his club. He might even have one for school as well, although they were less frequent. If he wasn't playing he would be bowling in the garden. The rejection had spurred him on rather than dented his confidence. Cricket is not just a summer sport and once the season was over he had a small break before winter training and district courses began. Every week we would find ourselves in a school gymnasium for indoor nets and on top of that he wanted to do extra courses that were being offered by Lancashire in their indoor nets. I know that children have to understand the meaning of no, but I felt powerless to prevent him from doing what he was loving and equally his drive and determination, and that also applied to so many other talented boys who were on these courses, had to be encouraged.

THE LOVE OF THE GAME

He progressed through each stage on his journey to achieving his dream of playing for the county, until we were left with one final hurdle. The trial matches. All the boys who had got through the various tests were now required to meet up on three different days to play each other in a series of games attended by the county coaches. The boys would be assessed on their performances and the best ones would form the county Under-11 side for the forthcoming season. It is important to reiterate that the boys were the ones being assessed because if you had watched the behaviour of some of the dads you would have thought it was them on trial for the county.

Chapter 19

I thought we had arrived in good time for the first game but as we emerged from the hedge-lined car park we were greeted by several of the boys being put through their paces. Not by their coaches but by their dads. Some of the dads had bats in their hands, some were bowling at their sons, some were doing fielding drills. I had a sense of foreboding. I knew what was coming.

'Can you give me some throw downs please, Dad?' he asked, understandably not wanting to be left out of the rather chaotic action taking place on the outfield.

'OK,' I agreed, when really I just wanted to find a nice solitary spot for my collapsible camping chair (a must for any cricket parent) and open up my Thermos flask. 'But don't smack them.' Restraint and self-control are not qualities often found in eleven-year-old boys and he duly smacked a few of the early balls I threw at him, narrowly missing parents, prospective teammates and coaches alike. This then caused an argument.

'I said don't smack them.'

'But it was there to be hit.'

'That's not the point, is it? There are loads of people around, it's dangerous.'

'But I have to warm up and I can't play defensively if it is a ball I can smack.'

'Don't smack any more.'

'OK.'

He remembered that instruction for all of the next two balls I threw at him before launching another.

'Right, that's it. No more.'

'Oh, Dad.'

'No, Ben, you will hurt someone and we can't have that.' Although if he had scared the dad bowling perfect leg breaks at his son, who was responding with some perfect defensive shots, I wouldn't have complained.

Ben stomped off, I stomped off. We were both in the perfect frame of mind for what lay ahead. As the boys gathered round the coaches to receive their instructions for the day, I headed back to where I had left my chair. To my horror it had been surrounded by other chairs, with other parents sitting on those chairs. My chair was in the middle of this throng. I couldn't just pick it up and move it. I was going to have to remain as part of a parental group for the foreseeable future.

Ben's team were batting first and he was way down the order so all I had to worry about was drinking my coffee and not getting infuriated by the conversation swirling around me. I was sitting in the know-it-all section. No sooner had the game begun than the details of each boy involved were being openly discussed.

'This lad opening here was great last season. He was only out once in the whole of the summer. Every other time he had to retire,' said a dad who had appointed himself as the fount of all knowledge.

'Oh, does he play for your club?' asked one of the dads.

'No no. I was just talking to one of the coaches beforehand. He's got to be a shoo-in for the county.'

Immediately panic spread round the parents of other batsmen in the game.

'You mean he's already been chosen?'

'Surely they aren't judging it on last season?'

'Won't it be about what happens in this game?'

'Why have they been running courses all winter if they have already decided who is in and who is out?'

Two or three were immediately up out of their seats and away to talk to their sons, who would be batting over the next hour or so. I wouldn't have been entirely surprised if they had suggested that they try run out the really good batsman to make sure he didn't get a big score. It felt that competitive.

The fount of all knowledge was not done. 'The boy bowling at the moment, he played for the county last year, so you would think he would be selected again.'

'How could he have played last year?' asked one of the other parents.

'Well, he got in a year young last season,' continued the Fount, 'so you would have thought if he was a year younger than every-body last year, that he would keep his place in a squad full of lads his own age this year, wouldn't you?'

I didn't want to be involved in these conversations but that didn't mean that they weren't affecting my thought process. *'So if this lad I'm watching here,'* I was thinking, *'was in the squad last year and will be in the squad this year then that's one less place available to Ben. Ben might have to out-bowl him to stand a chance here.'* A matter of overs into what was going to be a very long day and I was already worrying and my competitive hackles were well and truly up.

The Fount continued, offering thoughts on the wicketkeeper, the spin bowlers and the fielding. He had been around the county set-up for a while as he had other children who had gone through the system and his boy in this age group had been earmarked at an early age as a talented cricketer. He was quite happy to offer this information to us as well. Occasionally he would pause from regaling us and take himself off to talk to one of the coaches standing near the pavilion, leaving a trail of panicked parents in his wake. I know psychological warfare plays an increasing part in the modern sporting world, but I wasn't expecting it to be used on a group of parents at a cricket match.

We all ended up, at different intervals, going over to talk to our sons who weren't on the field of play, me included. If the other parents were anything like me then they went over on the pretence of going to reassure their child, when in fact they were looking for reassurance for themselves. I would head to the pavilion as nonchalantly as I could and at a point when the Fount wasn't talking about bowlers. I didn't want him to think he had got under my skin. Which he had. Of course. I'd saunter over to Ben.

'You OK?'

'Yeah, fine.'

Silence. He was watching the game and didn't have a great deal to say. I was watching the game and wondering how I could get him to reassure me! He also didn't want his dad hanging around while he was with his mates. The silence lengthened.

'So,' I began, 'how do you think it's going?' Reassure me here son. Tell me that you think the other bowlers aren't up to your standard. Please.

'Well, I haven't done anything yet, have I?'

It was a good point. He hadn't been on the field, the game hadn't been going on very long and he had just been chatting with his friends.

'No, you haven't, that's true.' I was searching for another angle. 'But what do you think of what you've seen so far. Standard's OK, isn't it?'

'Yep.' Not only was I not being reassured, I was being stone-walled by a monosyllabic boy who didn't want to talk to me.

'Do you know many of the boys who are out there at the moment?' I queried, and then deciding to ditch any subtle angle of questioning. 'Any of the bowlers, maybe?'

'Yeah, a few.'

'And?'

'And what?'

'And do you feel confident that you are better than them?'

'Yeah, yeah.'

I'm not sure I reassured either of us. I probably made it worse by reinforcing to my son that he was in a battle with these other kids, when I should have been using our old mantra of 'just enjoy it and have fun'.

I wasn't having fun though. The Fount was still blathering on, my son wasn't on the field and, as every parent knows, when only one of you is at a game you have to provide updates, plenty of updates, for the other one . . . even when nothing is happening concerning your own child!

Buzz, the first text arrives:

How is it going? xxxx

We've only just started!! xx

Is he ok tho? Happy? xxxx

Yes, he's fine. xx

What's he doing? xxxx

Nothing. xx

Nothing? How is he going to get picked if he isn't doing anything?
xxxx

Don't worry. His team are batting. He'll bowl later. xx

Thirty minutes later. Another buzz.

Is he ok? xxxx

Yes he is still ok!!! xx

Are you ok? xxxx

Yes. I'm ok. xx

Even though I wasn't, as I was busy dealing with text updates, the Fount, my son not wanting to talk and my own nerves. The pattern continued for a good three hours, the length of the innings for the first batting team. I was on a hamster wheel, constantly scrambling over know-it-all comments, pointless texts and boy grunts. It was a long morning of what was going to be a long day.

Cool boxes were opened, M&S food eaten by the parents, curled sandwiches on trays eaten by the boys. The coaches huddled together away from the crowd, comparing notes, and, once they were spotted doing so, parental necks craned in that direction. I half expected somebody to lob a sausage roll towards them, claim that they had dropped it and then go over to pick it up in the hope of hearing some nugget of information about their son. The resumption was ten minutes away when I sidled off for another chat with Ben.

'Feeling good?'

'Yeah.'

'What did you have to eat?'

'Sandwiches.'

That silence was coming again.

'OK. Well, bowl well.'

'Thanks.'

'And have fun.'

Churchillian, I am sure you will agree.

He wasn't being monosyllabic and surly because he was 'approaching that age'. He was being like that because he was nervous. Very nervous and understandably so, certainly more understandably so than yours truly. He didn't open the bowling.

His side now bowling. He's not opening though. xx

Oh no. Is that bad? That's not a good start is it? Poor love. Is he ok? xxxx

Am sure it will be fine. He looks ok. xx

Was I trying to reassure my wife by saying it would be fine, or was I trying to reassure myself? I think we all know the answer. Everything that was being said around me was mere background noise. I wasn't paying any attention and was just keeping my eyes on Ben, trying to gauge how he was. Also the Fount had run out of people to analyse so he was beautifully silent. Eventually, after what had felt like the longest day of my life, he was thrown the ball. This was it, his big moment to impress and get himself into the county set-up; something that had been his aim for the last eighteen months or so.

Such is my pessimistic nature that as he began his run up for that first ball my overriding thought was *'please don't get hit for four or even worse six'*. I wasn't thinking *'go and get a wicket with your first ball.'* I just wanted him to have a nice gentle start. And he did. The batsman put bat on ball with his first delivery but in a defensive way, no run was scored and I breathed a huge sigh of relief. Two more balls followed, nothing remarkable with either, and then he ran in with his fourth delivery. He released the ball and the batsman took a step forward. He put his bat in front of his front pad and prodded at the delivery. The ball thudded into the bat and looped up in the air back towards Ben. He had completed his follow through and now had his eyes on the ball as it soared towards him. He was going to have to take a couple of steps forward to catch the ball so that when it went into his hands they would be just in front of his knees. And the ball did go into his hands. And then it came back out again, and landed gently on the cut, brown grass at his feet.

There were oohs and aahs from around me. There was a sigh of relief from somewhere too, probably the parents of the batsman. I felt several pairs of eyes on me but I made sure I kept looking straight ahead. I couldn't make eye contact with them. I didn't take my eyes off Ben and I am glad I didn't because he bent down and grabbed the ball off the ground with a big smile on his face. He knew the batsman at the other end, they were at the same club, so he had a joke with him. He walked past the umpire and said something to him and as he walked back to his mark to begin his run up he looked at me and just shrugged. I was feeling gutted on his behalf and yet he appeared to be writing it off as just one of those things. Surely it should be the other way around? The rest of his over was uneventful and as he jogged back to his fielding position, some of his teammates patted him on the back and offered words of encouragement. The parents around me were asking if I was OK and telling me it was just one of those things. While the boys were getting on with it and enjoying their game, the parents were analysing it.

Two weeks later, after he had played in all three trial days, the letter arrived. He wasn't confident as he hadn't put on a stellar performance on any of the days. The letter was addressed to us, the parents, so with Ben at school and the house to myself I opened it; and then I burst into tears. He was in. He had been selected for his county. The tears were relief, I suppose, on my behalf, but also just sheer delight for him, knowing he had got something he wanted, that he was one step further towards his dream. His mum shed a tear too when she found out, but Ben, on the other hand, smiled, did a fist pump and went off to play on the PlayStation.

He is now in his third year of playing schoolboy county cricket and given that he plays for his school and his club as well it feels that our summers are dominated by this sport. Our winters too, actually, because of all the indoor nets he does. I marvel at his coaches for their knowledge and patience and how they have developed him. I marvel at the unheralded ground staff around the country who provide the excellent wickets on which they play and the volunteers at the clubs who provide food for the boys. I marvel at the boys themselves for the standard of cricket they are playing and I marvel at Ben's younger sisters who get dragged along in all weathers to watch an awful lot of cricket and who put up with it, even if it can't be much fun for them.

The weather plays its part in the lack of fun. When we began our cricketing journey, we envisaged spending long afternoons in the sun with a cold beer watching our son, while our daughters cartwheeled on picnic rugs next to us. In reality we spend most of our time huddled together in biting winds on grounds with little protection from the weather, with picnic rugs over our freezing bodies rather than on the floor next to us. A summer sport does not mean a sunny sport in the UK.

While I am happy to huddle together with my family when it is cold, I still need that solitude at times during a match, particularly when Ben is bowling. Cricket is an odd sport in that while it is a team game, the battles within it are essentially individual ones. Football and rugby move so quickly, for example, that while each game may witness individual brilliance the spotlight never focuses on one player for too long. A penalty is probably the only occasion where it becomes one versus one. Cricket, on the other hand, is based around one batsman taking on one bowler. So when that batsman or bowler is your son, you feel like you need nerves of steel to cope. International cricket is littered with stories of a batsman hitting his first century or a bowler winning a close match with a parsimonious final over and the parents not being able to see it. Not because they weren't at the ground or weren't watching the television but because they physically couldn't put themselves through it. They might have been at the ground but they had to take themselves to a part of it where the pitch wasn't visible, or the game was on television but they went out for a walk to try to calm themselves rather than watch it. We are obviously not at that level in our little world but I can understand those feelings. Sometimes I feel like I have to force myself to watch, particularly if it is close like the Yorkshire game, but always I need the peace and quiet and to be alone with my own thoughts when he grabs that red cherry and begins his run up.

No matter what the level of the match, I need to be isolated from the crowd. Ridiculous as it sounds, I feel like I am living every delivery with him. In reality, of course, it doesn't matter to me whether he gets hit for four or six or takes three wickets in three balls. But it matters to him, and even though you tell yourself that all children need bad days and difficult things to happen to them so that it prepares them for life, it is bloody hard as a parent to watch them suffer. It becomes even harder when you are joined by other people. I find that no matter how hard you try to be on your own, groups of people will always join you because there will always be a group of dads who 'walk the boundary'. They can't help themselves. They can't sit still for too long and every half an hour at any amateur game you will see them stroll the ground's perimeter, chatting, analysing and putting the world to rights. And then they reach me. All I want to do is watch the game, all they want to do is analyse what is going on.

'Bowling well today, your lad.'

'Yep.' I'm now the monosyllabic one in a two-way conversation and thinking I don't want to praise him too much because I don't want to be boasting about him.

'Think we need to restrict them to a hundred and forty.'

'Yep,' I reply, but thinking *how on earth do you know what a good total is because we haven't played at this ground before and we haven't played this team before*'.

And then if it isn't going well someone might pipe up, 'He's bowling a bit short today isn't he?' or 'He needs to be swinging it more today, doesn't he?'

'Yeah, maybe,' I grunt, thinking at the same time that he is eleven. Are we really going to stand here and pick apart every delivery as if we were on *Test Match Special*? Evidently we are, because they'd then tell me they'd spotted a weakness in the batsman and that maybe Ben should be doing this or doing that to exploit it and that I should tell him the next time he came down to field near me. I don't do that. I simply nod and put that thumb up after every over to encourage him and let him work things out for himself.

He played in a school cup game for an older age group, because they have no qualms about players testing themselves against older, bigger players in cricket, unlike football. The opposition's coach had constantly moved his side's field and chosen the bowlers when Ben's team had batted. As the opposition chased down the runs, it was building up to an exciting climax. Our coach let the boys do everything themselves. They made all sorts of mistakes as they put fielders in the wrong spots, tried to keep one batsman

on strike and rotated the bowlers. Not once did the coach inter-
vene. They lost on the last ball. Some parents weren't happy and
the boys were very upset, but as the coach told them, they would
be stronger for it. If they were in that situation again, they would
cope with it better.

I think I am getting better at dealing with the nerves. For some
club games, I have even scored to take my mind off it. Scoring in
cricket involves noting down every single delivery from both a
batting team and a bowling team's point of view. You need top
powers of concentration, huge mathematical nous and a knowledge of the players on your own team. I am lacking in all areas
but it gives me something to do, although future generations
may look back at some scorecards from the twenty-first-century
Cheshire League and realise that they don't always add up.

The nerves don't just come in the cricket with Ben, they come
in every swimming race with Jessie, because that is the sport that
matters to her. That is the one she wants to succeed in, go to
the Olympics in. I can't even score in that to take my mind off
it, in fact I can't even go for a walk in that sport to take my mind
off it. I just have to sit there with a sick feeling in the pit of my
stomach. If something goes wrong for Jessie in the swimming, it
all happens very quickly and it is over. If she has a bad race then it
doesn't linger for hours and she is quite pragmatic about dealing
with it. If something goes wrong for Ben in the cricket, he can
stew on it for the whole day. A bad bowling spell can affect his
body language and his mood for a long time. He'll be stomping
around the outfield, he'll be kicking the turf at his feet in anger,
he'll be avoiding all eye contact with me and his mum. And while
he is displaying this petulant behaviour, my dad will sidle up to
me and say . . .

'He's just like you, you know.'

Chapter 20

The room was wood panelled. It was dark wood and heavily varnished so it felt like the room was closing in on you. Gold-framed photos of past and present dignitaries from the organisation I was visiting lined the walls. The carpet was worn and had seen better days and for a venue that was doing its best to create an illusion of grandeur, the tables before me were flimsy and basic. Four chairs had been laid out for myself and the two other people entering the room to sit down on, plastic bucketed things that again seemed incongruous with the surroundings. Three men beckoned us towards the chairs as we came through the door. Three men who just like the carpet had seen better days. It would only be a guess, but I would suggest the average age of the three would have come in just shy of eighty.

The three of us sat down, all of us suited and booted, just like Statler and Waldorf and their friends opposite us. I had never met the men opposite, but I knew the two people who were alongside me. One was a teammate from the football club I was playing for and the other was the referee who had sent me off in our last game.

'You are here to appeal your sending off in a game played on the [and then they gave the date] and subsequent punishment. Is that correct?'

This was already feeling a lot more serious than I thought it was going to be or in fact needed to be. 'I am,' I replied, half expecting Rumpole to come out from behind one of the wooden panels.

'Well, we will now ask you and your teammate to leave the room. We will ask the referee here for his version of events. We will then ask you to come back in with your version of events and if your teammate has anything to add he can then do so. Now please leave so we can talk to the referee.'

So, having just sat down, we got up and left. It sounded like we could be in for a long evening, which was a concern as at least one member of the judging panel didn't look like he had long left. We waited outside the room while the referee tried to make me sound like an appalling member of society. Sorry, while the referee gave his version of events. His account didn't take that long and soon we were turning side on to each other so that we could all pass through the doorway. Him on his way out, us on our way in.

Once back in the bucket seats, the man in the middle of the three put his point to me. 'The referee, in his report in front of me here, and in his testimony in this room, has sent you off for calling him a clown. Is that correct?'

'Is that correct in the sense that that is what he has told you? Or is that correct in that that is what I admit I said to him?' I'd watched a bit of *LA Law* and would have quite liked to have been a barrister if I had been smarter so I was relishing some adversarial combat. A regional FA disciplinary appeal probably wasn't the best place for it, particularly as I was hoping for understanding and leniency.

'The latter, Mr Chapman,' came the reply, with a sigh of exasperation. 'Did you call the referee a clown?'

'Well yes and no. I used the word but in context.'

'Please explain.'

I had a sense that my teammate was trying to stifle a laugh next to me, but I didn't want to look at him in case that caused the stifle to fail and the room to be filled with giggling. That wouldn't have helped my cause.

'The game had finished and having lost we were going through the usual post-match niceties, three cheers for the opposition and shaking hands. We then pulled off to the side of the pitch as a group to have a chat about how the game had gone. The referee, seeing that we were having a team meeting, started to walk off the pitch with the match ball. He chose to wait for us by one of the corner flags. As we continued our debrief, I could see the referee attempt some keepyups.'

'Keepyups?' said one of the three, who might have just woken up.

'Where you try to keep the ball in the air as long as possible using your feet, your legs, your knees, your head.'

'Thank you.'

'Anyhow, he wasn't particularly good at keepyups and as our meeting finished I walked over to him to collect our match ball and shake his hand. I took the ball, took his hand, shook it and said "thank you, well reffed, even though I thought some of your decisions were not exactly correct."'

And by the way, I know you are reading this and thinking, *'Really? You said that to him in such a nice, polite way and didn't swear at him?'* and I can honestly tell you that yes, I *was* polite and no, I didn't swear.

I continued. 'And he replied to me "Well, I'm the referee and my decision is final." To which I said "Well, judging by the way you were juggling this ball, I thought you were a clown rather than a referee."'

It didn't go down well in the room. It didn't go down well with the referee. 'At which point, he immediately took out his red card and told me he was sending me off. After the game. I don't deny I used the word clown, but it was part of an admittedly not funny joke and I don't think it warrants the punishment I've been given. A thirty-three pound fine and a six-week ban seems slightly excessive.' I still think my teammate was trying hard not to laugh.

The panel all had their heads down and were scribbling on notepads in front of them. I couldn't see what they were writing but I imagine the word *clown* was written in big letters and underlined several times. They muttered to each other before one of them addressed us. 'Anything to add?'

'No,' I replied.

'Either of you?' he continued, looking directly at my teammate.

He just shook his head, because if he had opened his mouth that stifled laugh would have filled the room. We were then invited to step outside while they made their decision. Back in the corridor, I nodded at the referee. He nodded back. I wanted to roll my eyes at the ridiculousness of the situation, but feared he might see that as a show of dissent and produce a yellow card from the breast pocket of his suit. The red card didn't really bother me because it was shown to me after the game and therefore hadn't affected us, but I did object to the fine and the automatic length of the ban for what I considered a minor offence. Professional players don't get six-week bans unless they have done something utterly abhorrent and I didn't think and still don't think that using the word *clown* is abhorrent. Remarkably the establishment ended up agreeing with me and reduced the fine and annulled the suspension so that I could continue playing. We all shook hands in the room, referee included, and agreed to put this 'incident' behind us. Just before I was allowed to leave the room, I was warned about my future conduct. I ignored that warning.

We live in a footballing era where Barcelona have set the standard. It is all about the beautiful game. It is about 'tiki-taka', Lionel Messi, flicks and tricks, players gliding across the turf, wonder goals, skills, tekkers, sensational through balls, backheels, nutmegs, sleeves of tattoos and immaculate hair that is in the same position in the ninetieth minute as it is in the first. I grew up in an era where it was all about work rate, tackling, heading, passion and chugging through mud, where the only tattoo might have been a faded heart with an arrow through it on the forearm of a grizzled veteran. Hair wasn't gelled or waxed off chests, it was allowed to 'flourish'. This isn't a sepia-tinted lament that it 'was better in my day'; it is in some way trying to offer an explanation of my footballing education. Ever since I was moved out of goal to play, I was always encouraged that if the ball was there to be won I should go and win it, and if it meant clattering somebody in the process of winning it then so be it. That was just the way the game was. Despite that forty-yard goal – yes, I'm still mentioning it a couple of chapters later – I still maintain there is no greater feeling than a thumping header or a thundering slide tackle that takes both ball and man. The purists will roll their eyes, and might well suggest I'm a Neanderthal. My son has done it several times over the years, particularly when I have tried to get him to practise tackling or heading and all he has wanted to do is work on his 'rabonas', 'around the worlds' or 'waka-wakas'.

How can standing on the ball and spinning a hundred and eighty degrees or chipping the ball from behind your standing foot give you the same feeling as sliding several yards through puddles and mud to win the ball and knock someone over in the process? Ben, of course, puts the question the other way round. What I was never encouraged to do was mouth off. That was my own stupid fault, every single time I got into trouble. There were yellow and red cards at university for mistimed tackles, blatant professional fouls and the odd header that might have cleaned someone out in the process, and there were yellow and red cards for dissent. I just couldn't help myself. Having listened to the renowned sports psychologist, Dr Steve Peters, a man who has worked with some of the biggest sports teams in the world, this could be down to my Inner Chimp. The Inner Chimp is the part of the brain, so the theory goes, that sometimes we can't control. It can be impulsive, emotional or neurotic. The successful athletes are the ones who can control their Inner Chimp at crucial moments. So my disciplinary problems could be down to my Chimp or more likely they are down to me being a bit of a dick. And I was a dick a lot.

Three or four years after the disciplinary hearing over the clown comment, I was facing another long ban. I wasn't a kid when I went before the panel and I was even more long in the tooth when I took receipt of a referee's report and accompanying FA letter to inform me I was being suspended for eight weeks with another fine to pay. I had been sent off the week before for two yellow card offences. For the first one, the referee had deemed that I had taken an opposing player out as I went for a header and for the second one he had decided my foot was high when challenging for a bouncing ball, so as I connected with the ball my opponent's boot connected with my studs and he went down in 'agony'. It might have been a yellow card if I had been playing in a top flight game on the Continent, where they are notoriously strict about raising your boot off the ground, but I was expecting more leniency on a wet, muddy, bobbly playing field in West London, where the grass hadn't been mown for a month. So two yellows and I was off. Now, you are probably thinking *'an eight week ban and a fine for a couple of mistimed challenges seems unusually harsh'* and you would be right. After all, it is a longer ban than the straight red I received for the clown comment. However, I don't think the length of the ban was down to the yellow cards. I think, and I may be wrong here, that it was down to something else that the referee included in his report.

'Mr Chapman left the field after receiving the second yellow card and stood on the touchline where he proceeded to do "wanker" signs at me for the remainder of the game.'

Yep, that was what probably did it. As I say, I could be wrong, but acting like a petulant teenager on the touchline rather than accepting my punishment more than likely got me the eight-week ban. I didn't appeal because firstly it would have been excruciatingly embarrassing to have to explain my behaviour and secondly I deserved the ban. There is an argument to say it was quite lenient and I had got off relatively lightly. My Inner Chimp was costing me money and playing time.

Ben had been pestering me about coming to watch me play, which obviously he couldn't do if I was spending large parts of the season suspended. I wanted to be able to take him along to one of our games because I knew how much I wished I had watched my dad play rugby when I was growing up and at the same time I wanted to protect him from the bad behaviour, mainly mine, that went on at our games. Did I really want this six-year-old boy to witness the swearing, mainly mine, and the tantrums, mainly mine? I needed to have a strong word with my Inner Chimp before taking Ben along. With that duly done, and more importantly me dropping down from first team level to the second team, where the standard wasn't as competitive and therefore hopefully I wouldn't get as worked up, I took Ben along to a game.

On the journey there, I thought it important to manage his expectations. We had been to several professional games together and I didn't want him thinking he was on his way to watching something similar.

'Don't worry, I know you are not very good,' he said, before I could even get halfway into explaining the standard of football he would be watching. It was clear his expectations did not need managing. He was very sure in his own mind what he would be watching over the next few hours.

My mate Boney, with whom I had played football since university, had agreed he was going to bring his son along too. He was eighteen months older than Ben, but they were good friends. It meant they could have a kickaround on the touchline when they got bored of watching us, which they surely would. When we arrived, they both wanted to be part of everything that was going on. They wanted to be in the changing room pre-match, they wanted to hear the team talk, they wanted to run out with us and be part of the warm up. It was lovely to see and feel their enthusiasm, while at the same time sitting there with some apprehension, hoping beyond hope that nobody swore in the team talk because I really didn't want to go home and explain to Ben's mum why he now knew the word 'shit'. Everybody was on their best behaviour because of the boys and when we went out to warm up they were allowed to join in. While we huffed and puffed through our pre-match jogs and sprints, well, jogs and slightly faster jogs, they were warming up our goalkeeper. He even allowed them to score a few past him; well, I think he was allowing them to.

A couple of their shots might have just been too good for him.

We lined up as we always did, with Boney at right-back and me performing the role of the big lump up front. Having scored one goal in seven years at school and the odd one in four years at university as a defender, it wasn't my goalscoring record that had led the club to put me in attack, it was my nuisance value. I had scored a few, though, and I was hoping that on this day my own flesh and blood would be there to see me score and that he would be proud of me. For the first ten minutes or so I barely had a kick. The opposition were much better. The two boys weren't kicking a ball about, they were transfixed by the game. They would throw in the odd shout of encouragement as well. It was not to last.

With nobody around him and with barely fifteen minutes on the clock, Boney went down in a heap, clutching his buttock. One of his ageing muscles had let him down. He should have done some faster jogs in the warm up. We had a medical bag on the touchline but no physio. We didn't even have a substitute, so the boys saw an opportunity to get involved. As the referee stopped play so we could see whether Boney could carry on, the two of them sprinted on, their little legs galloping over the turf as they held one handle each of the medicine bag. Boney remained prone on the grass, hand on buttock. A couple of teammates hovered over him. I stayed on the halfway line because I didn't want to waste my energy jogging over to see if he was all right. Our two sons reached him and then proceeded to empty the bag all over the pitch. Some of the players helped put a few things back in but told the boys to leave out the cold spray and the sponge. They then proceeded to spray the spray in any old direction and drop the wet sponge all over Boney. Nobody else helped them as they didn't want to go near my friend's backside. Fifteen minutes in and my son wasn't watching me score goal after goal, he was helping his friend treat my friend's arse. It wasn't the way I had dreamt it.

Boney clambered gingerly to his feet. The hi-tech medical attention he had just received from a five-year-old and a seven-year-old hadn't had the desired effect. He hobbled towards me. Two minutes later he had reached me, only marginally slower than if he had sprinted.

'I can't go off because we've only got eleven.'

'What have you done anyway?' I asked, because it had been difficult to tell from the treatment exactly what part of his body he had injured.

'I've pulled something either in my arse or at the top of my hamstring and I can't run.'

'No change there then.'

'I can barely walk.'

'No change there then.'

Oh, the witty repartee between old friends.

'So, I'll come up front with you and switch a couple of people around.'

'But you can't move. I'm going to have to do the running for both of us,' I said, already worried that I was struggling with the running for one let alone for two.

'Well, I'll just try to play in the hole and set you up if I can.'

Playing in the hole is meant to be the position for the most gifted player in the team. The player with skill and pace. The player with the ability to see a difficult pass, with the ability to hit a searing shot if they have the time and the space. It is not the position for a man approaching forty with a damaged arse. He positioned himself in the centre circle and hardly moved for the rest of the game, while I puffed and chugged on alone up front. We each became more frustrated: him because he couldn't move, me because he couldn't move. And as we became more frustrated and more inept, our sons enjoyed it more. The early shouts of encouragement from the two of them had now been replaced by laughter and giggles. There was even a hint of sarcasm which, had it not been aimed at me and my footballing skills, would have evoked my admiration. They stood in the middle of our half-time team talk and our full-time team talk and they might have heard the odd swear word then. On both occasions we had a great big fat nil next to our team name. There was no glory goal from his daddy the first time my son came to watch, merely the opportunity for him to press a cold wet sponge on to Uncle Boney's bottom. On a positive note, at least I didn't get sent off.

'Did you enjoy that?' I asked him as we drove home, expecting a negative to come back and for him to tell me how bored he had been in the second half, when he started to have a kickaround with Boney's son.

'Yes, I loved it. It was so funny.'

'Funny? It wasn't meant to be funny,' I replied, with only half mock indignation. 'We were trying to win.'

'Yes, I know,' he continued, 'but Uncle Boney couldn't move and you weren't very good.'

He was being truthful. I wanted to press him further when he said 'you weren't very good': did he mean the whole team or did he mean me? I decided to leave it there because he probably meant me and even though he was correct it would still have hurt. I have always been a lumbering lump. Professional sport was never an option of course, but in my head it could have been and even if it had just been for one game it would have been nice for my son to have thought, *Wow, my dad is really good at sport.*

That was my last season playing amateur football. Jessie had arrived and with a combination of two children and London traffic meaning an away game could take up most of a Saturday, I couldn't really justify the time any more and Ben couldn't get a laugh at me trundling around a pitch. Veterans' football and cricket could well be an option but again they take up too much time and I hate to think I have got to that stage in life where I am a 'vet'. On moving North, a couple of men approached me as I watching my son's cricket match to say the over-40s league was starting soon and would I be interested. I was thirty-eight.

'Hard paper round?' they asked.

'Hard paper round,' I confirmed.

So I'm left with 'celebrity' charity matches as my only source of team sport and my children's only opportunity to laugh at their dad doing sport. I've played in cricket matches where I have suffered the yips and have not been able to land a ball on the wicket, knowing all the while that Ben would be in the crowd enjoying my discomfort and knowing that he could be doing better. I have been in a football match in the same team as Piers Morgan, taking on a One Direction XI, knowing that at least with Piers in the team I wasn't the worst player on the pitch, while also knowing that my daughter wouldn't be watching me at all and would in fact be cheering on Harry, Liam, Niall and the rest of the opposition. And woe betide you if you tried to tackle any of 1D in that game because if you did you had twenty-five thousand people booing you. I clattered Ronan from Boyzone in that match instead and nobody seemed too fussed about that.

'At least one of their goals was your fault, Dad. At least one.'

'Yes, but it's all for charity, so it doesn't matter really, does it?'

'Well, you looked pretty bothered about it at the time though. Were you shouting at the linesman because it was offside?'

'Yes I was. And I wasn't shouting, I was asking.'

'You were shouting.'

'Well it doesn't matter now does it? Anyhow, did you see my amazing tackle on Ronan from Boyzone?'

'No. I went to the loo.'

'And I didn't see it because I was watching Harry warm up,' piped up Jessie. 'We saw you get substituted though.'

Growing up I wanted to be the next Bryan Robson. Now I am grown up, I have morphed into Daddy Pig from the cartoon series *Peppa Pig*. I am a figure of sporting fun to my children, and not an all-action hero like Robson was. In these charity games, I am one of the ones who cocks up, I am one of the slower ones or one of the less able ones. Now that is partly because of age and partly because I am both alongside and up against ex-professionals in those sports. I was hardly in Robert Pirès' class when we were both in our twenties, let alone now, so when I am in the same team as him it is obvious that he is going to look ever so slightly more accomplished. And while I can accept Pirès being more accomplished than me, what is harder to come to terms with is my own children now being more accomplished than me and them knowing that they are too.

Chapter 21

'With my boy Corey, who is nine, I play chess,' Andrew Flintoff told Kirsty Young on BBC Radio Four's *Desert Island Discs* programme, 'but even now I find it hard to let him win. I do every now and then.'

'Well that's good of you,' Kirsty told the former England captain, with a giggle in her voice.

One of the greatest sportsmen of his generation then added, 'Well I think you have got to earn things. I'm a big one in earning a victory or earning something.'

In my opinion, it is an admirable theory and one that I wholeheartedly agree with. However, to allow your children to earn a victory, you as the parent need to have the ability to be able to control when they win and when they don't. I can thrash my two eldest children at chess, and I mean thrash them, if I so choose. I could thrash my youngest as well, but it seems somewhat cruel to beat a two-year-old at a game that requires mental strength and dexterity. The fact that it is based on mental ability is the reason why I can beat them so easily, the reason why I can control how I win or how I let them win every now and then. I am cleverer than them. Mentally I am much more developed. My brain has over forty years of experience built into it compared to their thirteen or eight years. In a game of strategy, where luck is absent, I am still the King in our house. Sudoku is another game in which I rule in the Chapman home. I'm probably quicker than them at word searches as well but, to be honest with you, being the best at Sudoku or chess is not something that is near the top of my ambitions. I still want to be the best at football, tennis, swimming and cricket in our house. I want to have the control to allow them to beat me, or to make sure that they suffer defeat to their dad so that they know how to lose. Although, as much as I tell myself that I want that control so that I can teach my children how to act in defeat, it really boils down to the stark fact that I simply don't want to be the third best at something in a household of five when the only people below me are a toddler and a wife who didn't do anything sporty at all until she met me.

My mum wasn't particularly sporty. Apart from the odd game of something or other in the garden she didn't seem to do much else in the sporting world, and those games in the garden became less frequent after that incident where my dad put her through the fence into next door's flower bed during a game of rugby. She would occasionally join in a family game of tennis and she would sometimes go off for a game of squash, always against the same opponent. She wasn't one for joining league ladders and playing competitive games. My dad would play squash every Sunday morning and I would sometimes go along to watch, particularly when the club built a new hi-tech court. By hi-tech, I mean it had a glass back wall which made it easier to watch, rather than hanging over a balcony trying to get a glimpse of the action going on below. To book a court, you had to stick a small stamp bearing your name on to a huge white grid with the courts running vertically and the times available going horizontally. If nobody had taken the slot afterwards then I knew I would be able to have a hit around with my dad. Equally if his opponent was late, I could have a hit around with him beforehand. This was more problematic however. Squash balls back then would have one little coloured spot on them. The spot was an indicator as to how bouncy the ball would be. If the ball had a yellow spot then that was the least bouncy ball when cold. It had to be really hot and warmed up to make it bouncy. That was the ball that my dad always played. So if I warmed up with him, he would find it incredibly frustrating as I had neither the power nor the ability to really get a rally going. We would end up having five or ten minutes of a ball rolling around the squash court with me chasing after it and him getting frustrated that I couldn't hit anything back to him. It would often end up with him having a rally with himself (the beauty of walls, eh?), both to get the ball warm and to relieve some of his frustration. I wonder whether his opponent was deliberately late sometimes so that he would have a riled man to dismantle when he got there.

Eventually, though, I did get better so that by the time I was approaching my teenage years I could hold a rally with my dad and I could get points off him too. Beating him was a different matter altogether. He had played squash for many years and I was hardly playing. Tennis had become my racquet game of choice. Partly because I wasn't too bad at it but mainly because I was approaching my teenage years and there were lots of girls who played tennis. We would play matches against other local clubs in mixed doubles teams. There were three pairs per club and you would play a set against each of the three pairs from the other club. I couldn't tell you about any single game from that period, nor whether we won cups or leagues or whether I received any individual medals. I could tell you, however, that my partner for the four years I played was Suzi White. Hers was the only girl's number I kept in my yellow Filofax and I never rang it to ask her out. The only 'love' in evidence was our score from time to time as my hormones raged and I struggled to control my serve with her standing at the net in front of me.

My hormones were probably making me a pain at home. I say probably because you try to pretend that you were a normal teenager back in the day, don't you, and not like the surly, moody, temperamental ones that you are having to deal with as a parent right now. I was probably being a pain to my mum and I would imagine I was belittling her in a sporting sense. She hadn't been banned for the moon boots as yet but we were not far off that day. So she challenged me to a game of squash. SHE challenged ME to a game of squash. I was starting to take points off my dad so how on earth did she think she would be able to beat me, even be competitive against me? So, one summer Sunday morning, rather than my dad book a court to play somebody else, he booked a court for the family. As he tried to keep my sister entertained, I attempted to beat my mum. I was cocky and cocksure. I would win this, I was sure of it.

Obviously, I didn't. My mum proceeded to dismantle me at the game. I tried to use power, she used craft and subtlety of touch. I was hitting shots that I would in tennis, she was using the angles of the squash court to maximum effect. I was getting more and more annoyed with myself, she was enjoying it more and more. I was taught a lesson, and not just a squash lesson. My mum had proved to her nearly teenage son that she wasn't a middle-aged, washed-up woman. That she did deserve respect and that sport wasn't just the domain of her son and her husband. In the heat of the battle and flinging my squash racquet around in temper tantrums, I didn't quite grasp the life lesson. I only understood that when I had calmed down from my defeat. Around two weeks later.

If my mum had beaten me at chess would it have been the same lesson? I doubt it. Did it have to be something physical at which she prevailed to prove a point to me? Probably. Is that the moment I am trying to create with my own children now? I think so. I need to be able to hit Ben for a four just so he knows his dad still has a bit about him. I need to crunch him in a tackle in the garden so that he knows he can't take the mickey and try to nutmeg me all the time. I need to score more points than Jessie in a netball game with her so she knows she can't win all the time and I need to power through the water at the last minute to beat her in a swimming race so that she knows where she has got some of her ability from. We leave gymnastics well alone. She knows she is better than me and knows she got none of her ability from me. Is it about teaching them or is it about me proving myself to them and to myself?

Traditionally boys are meant to like cars and bikes and things that go fast. They have never interested me, neither in a sporting way nor in a leisure way. I have never been bothered about the type of car I have had and I have certainly never wanted to own a motorbike. Sometimes I have had to get on a motorbike, a taxi bike to be precise, because they are a quicker and easier way to get around London than a normal taxi. Nerves among their passengers are normal so they tend to use what I would call reassuring drivers. Big, burly men who make you feel safe as soon as you clamber on behind and put your arms around them. There is a radio headset built into both your helmet and his so that you can have a conversation as you ride and so that he can put you at ease if necessary.

I was sitting behind one of these big, burly men one afternoon and as I had used the service several times by now I didn't need reassurance. We were talking about the usual things, sport, kids, more sport, when he started telling me about his son.

'He's fifteen and nearly as big as me.'

'So what does he play then?' I asked.

'He plays rugby. I used to play as well so he is following in my footsteps, but he is a big lad and he will only get bigger.'

'Frightening isn't it?' I said, using a word that we often seem to employ when referring to the growing-up period of our children. Frightening they are so big, frightening how fast they are growing, frightening that they are nearly as tall as me.

'It is. I think he is already stronger than me. Well, I know he is stronger than me. We were wrestling the other day . . .'

'You were what?' I interrupted.

'Wrestling.'

'Wrestling?' Every time I spoke to him it appeared to be a question.

'Yeah. Wrestling. Not in a Big Daddy sense or in an Olympic sense but just messing about as you do as a father and son. You know, just in the lounge, trying to rugby tackle each other and the like, getting each other in a headlock.'

'Oh. Right.' I was already fearing for the furniture in their lounge and I was expecting this story to end with a mirror falling off the wall or a stray foot going through a flat screen television.

'Anyhow, after about a minute of rough and tumble, I was stuck. He had got me in such a way that I couldn't move and whereas I would normally out-power him to get out of any trouble, I couldn't. I thought to myself I'm in trouble here. So do you know what I did?'

'No. Admit defeat maybe? Ask him to get off?' More questions.

'No. I bit him.'

'You did what?'

'I bit him.'

'You bit your own son?'

'I couldn't do anything else. It was the only way I could get him off me. I won't be wrestling him again, that's for sure.'

'Well he probably won't be wanting to do it again if his dad is going to sink his teeth into him.'

Wrestling or fake fighting is one of the few sports we haven't tried together. I may tickle him from time to time but as we enter the awkward, gawky teenage years he is such a mass of uncontrollable long limbs that I often end up being accidentally kicked somewhere painful and finish up in a strop with him. In fact our sporting battles now often conclude with one or the other of us annoyed. Usually me. To avoid this I try to make sure we take each other on in things I know I am going to win. So that is obviously chess, some more chess, and not much more.

We played golf on holiday a couple of years ago and I more than held my own. I ended up beating him quite comfortably. I was torn between trying to help him by offering advice ahead of each shot, and taking a small amount of enjoyment as he duffed another shot just a couple of yards. His frustration grew as the sun burned even hotter, and every now and then his anger manifested itself by him throwing a club across the fairway in frustration. Obviously this is not the done thing in golf, so as his dad I really should have told him off but at the same time I knew that the angrier he got the more likely I was to win. Also, as someone who has thrown squash and tennis racquets in my time, along with the odd golf club, not to mention the wanker signs at a referee, it could have been construed as hypocritical if I were to admonish him. Do as I say, not do as I did.

Pool and snooker, I win. These are pub games and he hasn't spent much time in pubs, so as someone who has I have an advantage. Darts is another pub game, but he has played that a lot and we encouraged him to do so because it helped his maths so much. I wish we hadn't. He beats me more often than not, or rather he succeeds in hitting double one before I do. We both try to stay cool during those times as we are holding sharp objects. Table tennis, we are even, tennis, we are even although I will win if I make him serve properly; those uncoordinated long limbs of his again serving me well. Skiing, he is faster than me, swimming, he is faster than me. And in those last two sports, where his sister is involved as well, she is using her brother as her spur to beat her dad.

Swimming races used to be so easy to judge when they were smaller. I knew whether to give them a length's head start or half a length. I knew how to time the race so that I would just go past them and win at the end if I was following Flintoff's law of making them earn a victory. I knew how to go past them towards the end and then slow down, look across through the spray and allow them to touch the wall first so that they won, if I was feeling generous. Then, without really noticing, I found the head starts I was giving them reducing in length until on our last summer holiday, the three of us had a race with Ben having no head start. Jessie had a length and we would swim three lengths and she would swim two. It was quite a generous lead to give to my, at the time, seven-year-old daughter, but I had clawed back that distance before. However, by the time I had swum a length, Ben was already clear of me and I wasn't making much headway on Jessie either. I knew I had to, as sportsmen and women are prone to say, go through the gears. I started to kick my legs furiously and power through the water using my arms, dragging the water behind me each time my hand entered it. As my daughter turned for her final length, I had a length and two-thirds to complete, Ben just under a length and a half. Although it felt like I was reeling in Jessie, Ben seemed to be stretching away.

I was going at full pelt. I wasn't thinking about timing a finish to let them win narrowly or gallantly lose, I was just thinking about catching them. I did consider swimming into Jessie as we crossed, to try to put her off, but remembered at the last moment that she was only seven. Ben turned with a length left and Jessie had less than half the length of the pool to go. My daughter's stroke never changed. She was calm, collected and correct, but Ben had started to sway ever so slightly and go in a crooked direction as he focused on catching his sister. I was all spray and thrashing and probably resembled a man trying to stop himself drowning. With half a length to go, I became aware of my wife filming this from the side and I realised that I was not going to catch either of them. Ben surged past Jess and she calmly touched the end to claim second as I arrived a couple of strokes behind. They looked over, all big teeth and gaps as they grinned at me. In between gasps of air I tried to return their smiles. Jessie, I could deal with. I had given her the head start and in future races would be able to adjust that, but my son and I had gone toe to toe. There was no head start. There was no slowing down to allow him to win. There was no control. I had no control of that race. He had beaten me fairly and squarely and he knew it. He was at an age where he was able to tell when I might have been letting him win so this meant a lot to him.

When he was younger, it used to be quite easy to let him win without him realising. I'd deliberately miss one of his deliveries so that he could bowl me. Letting goals past me in the garden was easy to do as was hitting shots into the net in tennis, so that he could win a point. Games on the PlayStation were another situation where if I wanted to win, I would. If I thought he needed a victory to boost his confidence I would let him win. I would go 2–0 up on a game of FIFA but then with the help of a comedy own goal or my goalkeeper trying to dribble the length of the pitch he would end up with a last gasp 3–2 victory. He'd run around the room with his shirt over his head, laughing and celebrating and we would have a rematch. That was then. Now every single game ends in acrimony.

I can't beat him. I can't beat him at any single game we play on the damned thing. We only play sport games on there; football, American football and golf usually. We have tried F1 as well but I can't keep the car on the track for more than five seconds. Now I don't consider myself an old man. I have grown up with computer games. I had a ZX Spectrum 48K in my bedroom from a young age. Technology doesn't scare me and I had a PlayStation before Ben was even born. I have wasted many hours, many months, maybe even years playing games and yet after just a few years of my son playing them, he has me over a barrel.

'Dad, do you want a game of FIFA?'

Before I even answer, I get a look from my wife. A look that says *'if you play him, play nicely. Do not lose your temper, do not accuse him of cheating, do not stomp off when you lose.'* Now even though she hasn't actually said any of that, I object to the *'when you lose'* bit. How can she be so sure that I am going to lose. Couldn't her look have said *'if you lose'*?

We have three beanbags in front of the PlayStation and the television. He takes one, I take one. One is pushed to the side.

'Who are you going to be, Ben?'

'I'll be Bayern Munich,' he says, while rapidly hitting the buttons on his controller to set up the game.

'Well that's not very fair, is it?' I am starting before the game has even begun and as if our roles are reversed and he is the parent and I am the child he asks, 'Why isn't it fair?'

'Well, because you play this all the time and I am not on it as much. So you are better than me, so can't I be Barcelona and you be Carlisle?' It is true, I am not on it as much, although I did once tell him our delivery of FIFA had been delayed a week when in fact it had arrived on time, but I wanted to practise while he was at school and without him knowing, so at least I had a head start. It proved futile. He still beat me the first time we played against each other.

He declined to be Carlisle and selected Bayern Munich. He chose Barcelona for me and in a blur of taps he was making changes to his side. He made five alterations while I was trying to make one. He scored within a couple of minutes of the game beginning. He didn't say anything, but instead turned his head away from me so I couldn't see his face. From the movement of his shoulders, his neck and his cheeks, I knew he was trying to stifle a laugh. He was trying not to laugh at me.

'How did you do that? How?'

'What? How did I do what?' I could hear the giggle caught in his throat.

'That bit of skill? What buttons do you press to do that?'

'I just did this, this, this and then that.'

'OK. Thanks.' I kick off and immediately try that bit of skill and instead of a controlled computer footballer doing what his did, mine just hoofs into touch. Like controlled footballer like controller of controlled footballer, you might suggest.

He laughs.

'Oh come on,' I moan like a stroppy teenager. 'Did you tell me the right buttons? You didn't did you? Come on, Ben, that's not fair. You have to help me.' Of course he has to do nothing of the sort and he is still laughing as he scores a second goal. I know that he did tell me the right buttons, it's just operator error. I may be computer able but pressing square, square, Left2 and triangle just to perform a step over is beyond my capabilities. And if you are twelve years old and reading this and are tempted to get in touch to tell me that a step over isn't square, square, Left2, triangle then please don't. I can't guarantee the sort of reply you would get.

The score goes up to 3–0, 4–0, 5–0 by half-time. Every time one of his players gets the ball, they surge past mine. Every time one of my players gets the ball and goes on a run, they are caught by one of his. We settle into the argument we have during every single match that we play of this game.

'Tell me what it is son, come on.'

'Tell you what what is?'

'You know. You know. There is some button or combination of buttons that you know that makes your players go ridiculously fast. When I have the ball, you always catch me. When you have the ball I can't get near you. What is it?'

'There isn't one.'

'There must be. This happens all the time. How can we have a fair game if I don't know all the buttons?'

6–0 . . .

'See? I just can't stop you. Are you enjoying thrashing me?' Stupid question. 'Would you not like a closer game?'

'I don't have any secret buttons. I just make sure I have fast players.'

Our voices, mainly mine, have been raised. His mum comes into the room and treats us both like small children.

'Why do you two play this? You never play nicely. If you have a secret button Ben, then tell him.'

'I don't,' he says adamantly, while still bloody grinning.

And as she leaves the room, I know he doesn't. I know he doesn't because I have Googled everything about it. I've looked on forums and websites and social media and there is no secret move, no way of making your players go so much quicker than the opposition. I want him to have a secret button because that would make the thrashings so much more palatable.

The score goes to seven and then to eight nil. We are in the dying throes of the game when I score. I finally score and then the game decides my player was offside. I forget where I am. I forget I am sat on a beanbag with my son nearby playing a computer game. The frustrations I felt when playing come to the fore and without thinking I throw the controller with some force into the spare beanbag as a rather loud 'Oh, fuck off!' comes out of my mouth.

'Maaaaaaaark' came an even louder scream from another room as my son rolled around in hysterics. Angry dad combined with swearing – it doesn't get much funnier for him, particularly with an 8–0 win in the bag. I think if my wife could have put me on the naughty step she would have done. Now, before we play on the PlayStation, not only are we told to play nicely but I am also told not to throw anything and not to swear. My son even takes pity me on now and will choose a lower league side to try to help me. The last time we played, his AFC Wimbledon side beat my Borussia Dortmund team.

Chapter 22

Arguing during games on Playstation, freezing and wet on a touchline as he has looked close to tears, car journeys arguing about the negatives and never discussing the positives, buying his first scarf to go to his first game, trying a new sport, splashing each other on holiday. I have taken it all for granted. The positives and the negatives of having a sporting son and being a sporting dad, the positives and negatives of being a sporting family of having weekends and weeknights defined by sporting activities. I have taken it all for granted. I loved sport and I played sport, so why would my children not want to? But what about if they didn't have a say in it? What about if it wasn't a case of not wanting but a case of not being able to? I have no idea what I would do then, how I would cope then. My friend does though. A man who works in sport, who plays sport, who loves sport. A man who is in many ways just like me. A man who understands the positives of sport, a man who is father just like me and a man who when he knew I was writing this book, wrote this for me:

Many sporting memories start with a sports day. Mine were always racked with nerves, desperate to do well, to a point where I made myself sick.

So it was an exciting time taking my three-year-old son Charlie to a local church sports day. Lots of excited kids bounding around, laughing, giggling – bundles of energy. My wife and I knew something wasn't quite right with Charlie, but he was young, probably just a bit delayed – and he was (is) a tall, handsome, athletic-looking boy. He'll be fine, I thought; sport will be his thing as it is mine. How can it not be?

We lined him up for the under fives' race – he was taller than all the other kids. He turned round and walked away. 'Come on Charlie – the finishing line is over there.' The other kids were waiting patiently, expectant, excited. I got him facing the right way – on your marks, get set, go. Off they go, zigzagging, chasing each other, crossing the finishing line, collapsing bodies into the arms of proud parents. Except one. Charlie stood on the start line, confused, upset, covering his ears. No one noticed, apart from me and my wife, who was walking back from the finishing line where she had waited to give our boy a big hug. We still gave him a hug.

That day is seared on my memory. It was the day I knew that the life I planned with my son was not going to be. I cried. I realise now they were selfish tears for what I would be missing out on. Missing out on the relationship I had with my dad which is still based pretty much around sport. I desperately wanted to do with Charlie what we did – long days at the cricket, away trips to Twickenham, Maine Road memories, mini-rugby. Best friends chewing the fat on sport, educating him and also, best of all, watching him play – our big beautiful boy rampaging round a rugby field. Proud parents watching him. (He was born in Twickenham, I always thought that would look good in the England rugby programme.)

We are over three years on from that day. Charlie was diagnosed with autism aged four but we always knew. In the last three years I have cried a lot. Trigger points everywhere. Seeing a father and son heading off to football, friends talking about the joy of coaching their son's rugby team or just seeing a kids' kickabout in the park. Apparently I was grieving; grieving for the loss of the life I wanted with my son. Self-centred grieving.

I could not enjoy my daughter's athletic achievements – it should be Charlie. Why can't it be Charlie?

Stupid and possibly an antiquated sexist viewpoint. I took my daughter to her first football game. I wanted desperately to enjoy it, and I did, but deep down, well not really deep down, I wanted it to be with Charlie, my son. That's what fathers and sons do, right?

I think perhaps that was a turning point – a slow realisation that I had to change. That it wasn't about me. I guess we all, as parents, at some point need to realise that it isn't about us. Whether our kids are potential world-beaters or not it is about them being happy. It is about them knowing you are there to support them, to hold their hand, to guide them, to love them.

I was told I had to redefine what 'perfect' was. Again a lesson for us all. Very few of our children will reach the very top, will succeed at the highest level. Some, like Charlie, will not even be able to take the first steps on a sporting journey. But he is perfect. And perfect for me is now making him happy, which at the moment is touring charity shops looking for old atlases, or scooting around the park, or climbing trees or bouncing, lots of bouncing, on a trampoline.

THE LOVE OF THE GAME

It still affects me seeing fathers taking their sons to mini-rugby or heading off to the football – previously it was like a sledgehammer to my stomach, now it is more like a pinprick. I have redefined perfect – it is Charlie.

AFTERWORD

Football in the garden or in the park is still our happiest domain; a kick about outside is always preferable to one controlled by shape-decorated buttons. Those early years of diving over balls so Ben could score and letting him nutmeg me are long gone. Now he can nutmeg me at will. Although when he does, he knows there will be a clattering tackle on the way that might land him on his backside. When he shoots at me, I am having to go full-length to try and keep it out, and try and keep it out I will. If he wants to score against me he'll have to earn it. He'll try and beat me in the air if we go for a header, but as I still have the height advantage I know that I will win those.

I stand in goal and watch him dribble the ball away from me; he does the odd flick and trick. Flicks and tricks that I could never do, and still can't do. He turns and runs towards me. I move out, I want to tackle him. Maybe I'll slide and tackle him. Yeah, that's what I'll do. Show him that for all the skills nothing beats a good tackle. I make my move. He makes his. His sleight of foot and mastery of disguise takes it past me. I am on the grass and I look up behind me, just in time to see him put the ball into the back of the net. He laughs and I laugh and I am reminded of the words of the great philosopher Phil Dunphy in the US comedy *Modern Family*.

In one episode he realises his teenage son has surpassed him in two of his passions, trampolining and playing the banjo. He begins the episode struggling to deal with it, telling his wife, 'I am as strong as ever. Certainly the strongest in our house.' But by the end, as his son bounces and tumble turns with greater dexterity and plucks away more tunefully, he has come to the realisation that he just has to deal with it. And his words in that episode go through my head as I pick myself up and go and hug my laughing son.

'Everything I can do, you can do better. It is not your fault. Every dad goes through it. The days you start seeing your son as a man and not a boy.'

The kitchen calendar is not hung up just so we can look at pictures of ourselves on a daily basis. It is there to plan our lives, or rather our children's lives. Without it we would be in trouble. Who is taking which child to what sport? Do we need to call in a grandparent or maybe even two? Is it possible to get from swimming to cricket in fifteen minutes? Will the smallest one mind being dragged around for four hours to watch a gymnastics display followed by a football match? Wouldn't it be easier if they didn't do quite as much?

I ask the last question an awful lot. I normally ask it as I am trudging to the car at half past six in the morning to take my son to a water polo session or as I am lugging six bags out of the car at nine thirty at night after gymnastics has finished. I think it in my head when I look at our bank statement and realise just what sport costs us. It costs us financially and it costs us horologically as well. Of course we are not unusual with regards to this. Parents across the land are in this situation too. There are always knowing nods across a car park as boots are packed or unloaded. Mutterings in queues as the chequebook comes out again to pay for the next three months of swimming. Nurturing your children in the sporting world takes time, money and love from a parental point of view, points that those who criticise the modern child for being lazy would do well to remember. In my experience the criticism itself is lazy.

They may be called the PlayStation generation but that doesn't mean that is all they want to do. Yes, they want to play on it, particularly if they can get their dad to swear, but all the kids I am seeing are craving physical activity. The lessons and sessions I attend with my children are full. Full of kids loving their gymnastics or their swimming, their cricket or their football. Full of parents willing their children on to do well, sometimes overstepping the mark maybe; but not out of malevolence, often out of misunderstanding. There are coaches from experienced to wet behind the ears offering up their time to bring on the next generation. Some are well qualified, some are using envelopes to pick a team. Without either end of that spectrum, our children would lose out.

Our children can play for fun. I make no apologies for constantly banging that drum of enjoyment and enthusiasm and laughter because as you progress through the world of children's sport, the enjoyment and enthusiasm is easily forgotten and fades away like images on an old photograph left out in the burning afternoon sun. They can play for camaraderie and they can play just in our hope that it tires them out and they will get a good night's sleep.

But if they are good they can develop. Since both the Olympics in London in 2012 and Rio in 2016, the sporting landscape appears to be changing. Families and children in particular are seeing that a career in sport doesn't just mean trying to be a footballer. Succeed in judo or netball, archery or gymnastics and you could be at a major games representing your country. Not only have individuals realised this, but the sports seem to have as well. There are more coaches, more competitions, clearer routes to progresssion and more advice. Pathways are in place to provide opportunities in areas that my generation wouldn't have even been aware about. Fitness and nutrition support and a warning about dangers on the way are all readily available. When I was growing up we were told smoking was bad for you and if you wanted to eat healthily then have an apple. They can have their own dietary plans and social media masterclasses if they reach a certain level in a certain sport now, and that's before they are even old enough to drive.

But I didn't want my three children to enjoy sport so they could be professional sportsmen and women. I wanted them to enjoy sport because of what it has given me. My best moments and my worst moments have come through my sport. My best behaviour and my worst behaviour (as you have seen) comes out in sport. My best friends have come through sport. To sit and have a beer with a friend and laugh about a game we played some twenty years ago is one of my great pleasures in life. They tend to walk off when I go further back and begin a conversation with 'Remember when I scored that goal from forty yards . . .'

My children have all of this to come. As they run around or fall over or win a race or fall off a beam or get hit for six, I wonder who they will be telling the tale to in twenty years' time over a drink. What memories lie ahead for them, what successes and failures are they going to have to cope with? I hope there will be more laughter than tears and I hope they don't get sent off as much as their old man did.

If they have their own children, only then will they realise what their mum and I go through weekly. Not wanting them to win every time but just wanting them to be happy. It is exhausting, but then all the exhaustion disappears when they look at you mid-activity and smile and turn to you after taking a wicket and put their thumb up at the same time you do. As they grow older they will play plenty of sport without me even being there but I hope they still tell me what happened, whether it is bad or good. I hope they still want to involve me in their sporting lives twenty years hence, whether it is playing and humiliating me even more or just going to watch. I still wonder how I have reached a stage in life where I go to games with both my dad and my son or daughter. How did that happen? It was only yesterday when he took me in a cagoule smelling of salt and vinegar crisps to the rugby union at Sale and yet now we are sat in my lounge watching rugby union on the television with my daughter in between us and my son outside practising his bowling.

Jessie asks my dad question after question about the rugby because she is loving it and thinking she might like to start playing it and that it would be fun to be in the scrum. My dad answers each one and then as she focuses on the game and the questions dry up, my dad looks over her head and out through the window and watches his grandson bowl.

'He's just like you, you know. I mean he's a lot better cricketer, but he's still just like you.'